The
Yankee Magazine

Richard M. Bacon

Book
of Forgotten Arts

SIMON AND SCHUSTER · NEW YORK

Copyright © 1978 by Yankee, Inc.
All rights reserved
including the right of reproduction
in whole or in part in any form
Published by Simon and Schuster
A Division of Gulf & Western Corporation
Simon & Schuster Building
Rockefeller Center
1230 Avenue of the Americas
New York, New York 10020
Designed by Edith Fowler
Manufactured in the United States of America

1 2 3 4 5 6 7 8 9 10

Library of Congress Cataloging in Publication Data

Bacon, Richard M
  The Yankee magazine book of forgotten arts.

  Collection of articles previously published in the
Yankee magazine.
  Includes bibliographical references.
  1. Handicraft. 2. Cookery. 3. Livestock.
4. Building. I. Yankee. II. Title.
TT157.B2   630   77-28761

ISBN 0-671-22824-2

Illustrations by Carl F. Kirkpatrick
Ray Maher
Margo Letourneau
Debra McComb-Wright

r

Table of Contents

USEFUL ANIMALS

FOOD FOR OUR FOREFATHERS

ARTS & CRAFTS

Preface

No matter where we live there are countless bounties to be gained by leading more self-reliant lives. Every so often there comes a surge of interest in country ways—particularly among people who are somewhere else—and a longing to recapture the simple pleasures of the past when living and the making of it seemed one. Partly this is pure nostalgia for another time, another place. But we have come too far to re-create an antique world even if we wanted to. And yet, the dream is a recurrent form of spiritual protest that can help us even now to combat the deadening effects of bigness and impersonal directives.

Today, wherever they live, many are acting to reorder their priorities. Selective knowledge from the past can help shape future goals and may release forces within ourselves we never knew we had. If riveted only to the here and now, we are all in danger of living only in the present, without heritage or future.

Too soon we let the experts rule our lives and thereby lose our sense of wonder. It is time to cultivate our inner resources once again. No need to blame others for the dreariness of a programmed life, if we see our life's work as a fair exchange for a questionable security to carry us along like the leaves on the surface of a pond.

Because no one is allotted more than twenty-four hours in each day, it is how one uses time that makes the difference. The countryman cannot escape routine for long any more than he can flee himself: there is wood to cut, animals to tend, snow to move, crops to plant and harvest, and meals to ready three times a day. There is endless maintenance both of buildings and personal relationships. Yet there is such a rich variety, that sameness is never so much of a problem as just learning how to cope with the multitude of competing demands that vie with the dictates of weather and environment.

Still, within routine there is time to stand and stare. To know the quiet comfort of a well-stocked barn, to amble up the hill pasture just to speculate, to swim in the pond after the heat and dust of haying, to sit relaxed and talk with friends, to dream up ways to make entertainment personal again—these are windfalls that renew a countryman's spirits.

On the way from house to barn I often pause to scan the heavens. So many signs could help us steer our lives if we were awake to them. Polaris does not guide the farmer to his chores—his feet would do that even if his eyes were closed—and yet it is there. Under these stars that overarch us all, there are infinite ways to keep alive a sense of wonder.

The Yankee Magazine Book of Forgotten Arts

The Homestead

Connecting a Wood Stove

(PLUS GOOD CHIMNEY CONSTRUCTION AND SAFETY RULES

Ofttimes, fashions that once seemed dated or even eccentric have a way of surfacing when they satisfy either whim or necessity. Such is the case for the wood stove today.

Dictated by economics, concern for supplies of fossil fuels, and nostalgia—heating with a wood stove has once again sprung into the public consciousness if only as a supplement for one's present heating system or to have as a standby in case of power failure, repeated fuel crises, or steeply rising costs.

Before you catch this fever of self-reliance, however, there are several points worth considering, any of which may quickly dampen your enthusiasm: the availability and cost of a functional, safe stove; a method of installing it in your home; and the labor and/or expense of amassing the wood necessary to make your investment pay for itself.

Many countrymen who properly cull their woodlots have never deserted the stove as the sole source of heating their homes. For them cutting and working up a supply of seasoned, split hardwood each year is an integral part of their life in the country. Others have hung on to a stove as an auxiliary space heater to tide them over before and after it is cold enough to justify turning on the central heating.

Even urbanites today—attracted to the idea of a supplemental heat source either from stove or fireplace—are finding a different and healthful kind of outdoor recreation (and a lot of hard work) in the process.

If you decide to go this way and heat with wood rather than add another layer or two of clothing and even retire earlier for the night, you must first find an efficient stove in good condition and then take all conceivable precautions to assure its safe installation and operation.

There is a wide variety of wood burning stoves available today as a result of the recent fuel crisis. Established companies that languished as anachronisms for the past quarter century have suddenly been propelled into greater production than ever and others have sprung up to duplicate ancient patterns or design boldly different ones. In addition, Americans have discovered foreign stove makers—principally from the Scandinavian countries. At one time their back orders stretched nearly as far as their distribution lines, but they are readily available now from many dealers in New England and at stiff prices.

For years the Franklin, potbelly, and box were the principal types of home heating stoves available. Some were beautifully simple; others were embellished with every possible type of ornamentation. Carefully tended and maintained, these have lasted for many years and many bear the labels of manufacturers long since passed into oblivion when central heating became fashionable and convenient. Some of the more recently made stoves will be fortunate if they see several seasons of use because they have been hastily designed, poorly constructed, and are made of metal that is questionable in its quality and thickness. Their only justification is their low price.

Before committing yourself, investigate all possible products. Compare costs, efficiency, and even looks. Then talk with other stove owners.

You may be fortunate to find an antique stove in mint condition. But be prepared to pay for it. Any stove should be free from cracks. It should have all its parts in working order. Replacement parts for old stoves are hard to find, but sometimes you can locate a local welder to restore the stove and manufacture new parts. Consider the color of the metal. A stove that has been operated unwisely by running it at continuously high temperatures will show metal discoloration on the firebox, which may have weakened its seams and composition. Although rust will appear on any stove unless it has been carefully tended, this is usually a minor problem and can be corrected with a wire brush, several coats of stove blacking, and concentrated work.

Prices for new stoves vary although all are higher than they were two years ago. Some may hesitate to spend as much as the $300 to $400 required for some American and many foreign made stoves. This can be translated into a considerable amount of fuel oil even at today's prices. However, buying a wood stove—like arranging for a home mortgage—should not be considered an annual outlay. Both can be depreciated for as long as they are functioning efficiently. Often the more you spend at this stage to assure safety, the greater the result in savings—possibly including your house and health.

Fire is always a lurking threat, even more so in the country where help is likely to be farther away. Therefore, safety is the most important consideration in converting to wood stove heating.

After you have decided on the stove to fit your needs, the next step is to see how it is to be vented. All solid fuel stoves must be connected to a chimney or flue to transport the smoke and gases outdoors. The prudent householder will see that this is done in accordance with safety standards cited by stove manufacturers, local fire and building ordinances, and the recommendations of the National Fire Protection Association.

Existing chimneys can often be used to vent a new stove. However, certain precautions must be taken first. Check the condition of the chimney. This can be done by the homeowner visually or by the local fire department. Look for stains on the masonry (these may indicate smoke leaks from former years), and loose or cracked mortar (a possible avenue for sparks that could destroy your house). Any defects should be properly repaired.

Clay mortar was commonly used in unlined chimneys built more than seventy-five years ago. It is questionable whether any of these meet present day safety standards, but the customary sight of smoke rising from a two-hundred-year-old chimney that has not been rebuilt or modernized attests to their continued use.

If the condition of an old chimney dictates it, you can hire a mason to rebuild it or at least insert flue linings in it. This will be a major undertaking and expense. Otherwise, chimneys can be lined with metal linings that are made to specification. Some homeowners have installed sections of regular stovepipe—fastened securely with machine bolts—by inserting them down the chimney to the stove connection.

Chimney tile—mortared together smoothly—or metal liners discourage the accumulation of creosote, which is one of the by-products of burning wood—particularly pine, cedar, and green woods—and which may ignite and cause chimney fires. (There are chemicals available that can be burned on the fire to discourage creosote accumulation. A safer way is to clean your chimney each year before the real stove season starts. Do this by wrapping chains in a burlap bag, tying a rope around its neck, and raising and lowering it against the insides of the chimney walls. Be sure you have blocked the hearth and flue openings before you begin. This will prevent soot from permeating the house.) Soot and creosote will be less likely to accumulate if you burn a fire continuously. These by-products are usually consumed satisfactorily but a visual inspection should be made.

If you use an existing flue for your wood stove, it should not be the same as that which is used for either the central heating vent or a working fireplace. Gases can be drawn downward and into the house while you sleep. For safety, therefore, you will have to make a list of priorities. Even if you decide to vent the stove through the overmantel of the fireplace, you will be giving up the use of the hearth as many did in the early days of "modernization" when wood stoves became fashionable and known to be safer and more efficient than fireplace fires. (Even the best fireplaces—while cozy and heart-warming—are only about 10 percent to 20 percent efficient in their conversion of wood to heat; stoves are from 30 percent to more than 80 percent in the case of some of the Scandinavian imports.)

Should you not have a chimney at all through which to vent a stove, or if blocking off an existing fireplace or even using it safely without extensive renovation is considered either hazardous or un-wise, you can beat the problem by installing a new chimney alto-gether. This can either be constructed of masonry (brick, stone, com-position blocks), which would call for the services of a mason and the resulting cost and bother, or a metal, prebuilt chimney. *Never* try to avoid the expense by venting your stovepipe through a win-dow sash. This merely courts disaster.

Masonry chimneys start from below frost level on a poured con-crete foundation and are built up; factory built metal chimneys, long known in the midwest and introduced here principally for sec-ond homes after World War Two, are supported from the roof and hang down.

Money, time, and labor are saved by installing a prebuilt chim-ney. Several nationally known companies manufacture them and provide specific instructions for installing them. These can be fol-lowed accurately by anyone with a feeling for tools and the ability to read directions.

Chimneys can be built either inside a house or made to run up an outside wall. The advantage of housing the flue within a build-ing is that of added choice of where to place the stove and more-even stovepipe temperatures. Unless the prebuilt chimney is inspected periodically during the heating season, the greatest disadvantage is that it brings the possibility of an unleashed fire closer.

Whatever kind of chimney you decide to install, make sure to observe the following points:

1. Stoves are heavy. Before bringing one into the house, check the underpinnings of the floor and strengthen them if necessary.
2. Wood stoves are radiant heaters. They must be kept at rec-ommended distances from all combustible materials. Wood, wallpa-per, many kinds of fabric, most kinds of paint, furniture, and even the woodpile itself are all potential fire hazards. A freestanding stove must be 36 inches from the nearest combustible material on

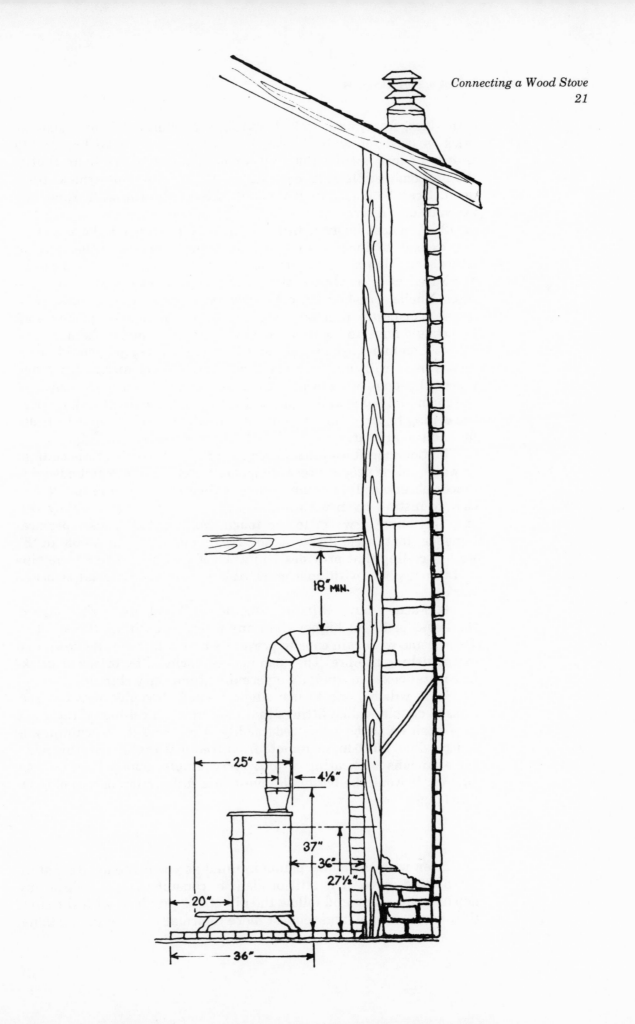

both sides, front, and back. If gypsum, plaster, asbestos, stone, or brick is used for wall sheathing, most stoves can be brought to within 12 inches from the wall. Some manufacturers state that if the noncombustible wall covering is 4 inches or more thick, their product can be placed as little as 6 inches from the wall. However, use your own discretion.

3. A noncombustible hearth should be provided under the stove and extend 18 inches out from the firing door, 12 inches out on either side. This can be a piece of asbestos encased in tin and can be purchased at a hardware store. Or you can make one of marble chips, shells, crushed gravel, brick, slate, etc., that is laid on a metal or asbestos firestop cut to the proper dimensions. Stoves on legs should have 18 inches or more of open space under them.

4. Common carbon steel or galvanized stovepipe should be 18 inches from walls and ceilings. The Shakers, ever an inventive and practical people, often located their wood stoves toward the center of the room and led a well-supported stovepipe at a slight angle under the ceiling to the chimney vent. This method provides added surface for additional heating.

5. Common flues must *never* pass through combustible ceilings or walls unless proper precautions are taken and recommended distances observed. Double and triple walled pipe are safe to use and easy to install. Even with a good fire going in the stove, they will only feel slightly warm to the touch. Manufacturers list specifications for clearances. If you do not use this product, cut a hole in the wall or ceiling that provides 18 inches of clearance around the pipe and fill this hole with noncombustible insulating material or brickwork.

6. Factory-built chimneys should be 2 feet above the ridge of the house or 2 feet higher than any projection within 10 feet of it. These come with rain caps to prevent water from running down and extinguishing the fire. They can also be enclosed by bricks or bricklike metal boxes to simulate a permanent masonry chimney.

7. It will be safe to use single walled stovepipe between sections of double-walled fittings that pass through ceilings if these are in a position to be inspected readily. However, if the chimney is inaccessible, built-in, or remote from frequent inspection, this additional means of heating a loft, for example, should not be considered. It would be better to invest in a full section or two of insulated pipe.

Even with the above points in mind as you contemplate installing a wood stove, it is still prudent to consult with your local fire department, study and follow the directions provided with the stove (if it is a new one), and request more information from the National

Fire Protection Association (470 Atlantic Ave., Boston, Mass. 02210).

ADDITIONAL READING
FOR INSTALLING AND OPERATING A WOOD STOVE:

National Fire Protection Association, "A Hazard Study: Using Coal and Wood Stoves Safely," 470 Atlantic Ave., Boston, Mass. 02210

Havens, David, "The Woodburner's Handbook," Media House, Box 1770, Portland, Me. 04104

Cooking on a Wood Stove

Wood cookstoves often have more individual quirks than the cooks who use them. But successful cooking with wood begins in the woodshed. The key to a well-planned and tasty meal is the availability and selection of fuel—split, dried and stacked perhaps a year in advance.

There are innumerable advantages to cooking with one's own wood. A twenty-acre woodlot will supply a family's cooking and heating needs almost indefinitely, if culled and harvested properly. The cost of wood grown on the farm is lower than that of any other fuel. In addition, wood cookstoves continue to function when outside power sources fail. They provide auxiliary heat, and this in turn can make a kitchen the family social center that modern efficiency has done its best to displace.

It is true that bread can be baked in any oven, but somehow the combined odors of fresh bread and a wood stove is enough to stir a pang of nostalgia in any breast.

However, before installing a wood cookstove in your kitchen—if you are fortunate enough to locate one in working order at a reasonable price—consider some of the *dis*advantages. Foremost is the amount of wood demanded by the cook to keep meals coming on time. If it is available and at hand, wood stove cooking is economical. But the constant cutting, dragging, splitting, stacking and carting of wood into the kitchen can be a tiresome task in a busy world and has persuaded many a farm boy to leave for the city.

Cooking with wood is dirty. Not only are wood ashes shifty things with wills of their own, but pots and skillets—especially if fitted into the lid holes for faster, hotter results—are miserable to clean and cannot be set on a countertop without leaving sooty rings.

Any wood fire in the home is a potential fire hazard; therefore, the chimney must be in perfect order and both it and the stove must be periodically checked and cleaned.

Finally—although a plate of biscuits in a wood stove oven is still only fifteen minutes away from the table when the men come in from 'coon hunting at 2:00 A.M.—cooking on a wood stove is not so quick, easy, and convenient as the modern gas or electric range. The wood stove has no place in a household where the cook has another job, unless it is either a second stove or merely a conversation piece. It takes a lot of damper-jiggling, stoking, and persistence to achieve satisfying results.

In learning the art of wood stove cooking—even if one is already a capable cook using another fuel—there are bound to be disappointments until the personalities of cook and stove become compatible.

To start with, the fuel must be dry. Although any wood will burn eventually, the fire will be hotter and more easily controlled if seasoned wood is used. Green wood can provoke chimney fires.

Hereabouts, the stove wood most generally used is white or rock maple, beech, white birch, and white or red oak. Ash is a fine wood, easily split and safe to use either green or dry. In the old days ash was used largely as kindling. It was split into ¾-inch vertical slabs, then these were worked into ¾-inch square sticks with a hatchet. Small-diameter ash was left in the round.

Countrymen never use pine, even for kindling. This wood can coat your chimney with resin, which in turn could lead to a house burning. Pine is saved for the lumber yard.

Wood that will not split easily because of knots or grain is stacked in another area of the woodshed and eventually finds its way to the parlor stove.

In the days when the wood range was king of the kitchen, country people kept a woodbox next to it, which was filled with a mixed lot of stove-length wood by the boys before they went to bed. From this the cook would select her fuel for the purpose intended: birch for a quick, hot fire with little body; maple and beech for longer-lasting dependability; oak (which takes longer to dry) for a slow, hot fire, once a bed of coals had been established. It was an unsplit oak log that was put into the firebox just before bedtime and banked with ashes. Usually the cookstove firebox was too small to hold a fire to last the night (a larger one would make it more difficult to adjust cooking temperatures), but some coals of oak would remain by early morning, which helped keep the chill out of the kitchen. During a spell of cold weather, the cookstove and parlor stoves

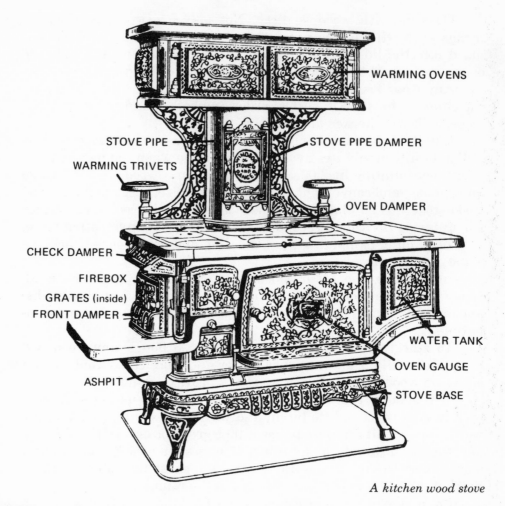

A kitchen wood stove

would have to be tended periodically throughout the night to keep the water pipes from freezing.

To kindle a fire, the housewife took a piece of newspaper, tore it down the center crease, and crumpled and twisted each half separately. She laid about eight twists on the grate, lighting both ends of one of them as she put it in, then loosely covered these with eight to ten ¾-inch square sticks of split ash. Within minutes her fire had started. Now according to what she was to cook, she selected fuel for her fire bed—often white birch and maple to get her chores off to a good start. (Any birch more than 2 inches in diameter should be split to dry in the shed; otherwise, the center will rot in a year's time and its usefulness will be lost. This is especially true of gray birch.)

Once the fire bed is established, the attentive cook spends her time regulating the drafts until the stove lids and oven are heated enough for her to proceed.

Most cookstoves have four different dampers. The front damper is located to the left and below the firebox. This is the primary source of draft, which allows controlled combustion. Ashes drop through the grate into the ashpit below. (It is here you can bake potatoes. Coat them with either grease or aluminum foil and turn occasionally until done.) The adjustable upper damper is called the "check." By closing the front damper and opening the check, you can cool the fire and save fuel. The regulation of the check is one way to keep a more even temperature in the oven while baking.

The stovepipe damper is the chief device for getting your fire going and, later, stopping it from burning too quickly and allowing an excessive loss of heat up the flue.

One other damper is important. This is the oven damper and is located either to the left or right of the stovepipe—depending upon the make—at the back of the stove. When this is open (as for starting a fire or cutting down the surface heat of the stove), the heat goes directly to the stovepipe; when closed, it allows heat to circulate across the top and around the oven walls before escaping through the flue. An open oven damper, therefore, spreads the heat more evenly under the surface of the lid covers.

The hottest spot on the cookstove lies between the left and center back lids in a six-lidded cookstove. When the oven damper is open, this generally shifts forward along the right ridge of the firebox. One of the great advantages of cooking on the surface of a cookstove is the cook's choice of temperature range. Results can be had instantly merely by shifting the pots backward and forward from hot to medium heat, far off to the right or left for warming or simmering. If the stove is equipped with a pair of warming ovens or movable trivets attached to the metal casing around the stovepipe, the cook has handy places to set her breads to rise, keep platters and food warm, dispel the dampness from salt, and hang dishtowels and mittens to dry.

Many cookstoves also boast a holding tank for water on the right. Not only is warm water available whenever the stove is going, but the added humidity is healthful and seems to temper the room's cold corners.

It is oven cooking that is the hardest to learn and the most challenging. The art of wood stove cooking is centered around the successful maintenance of oven temperature. Most stoves have a gauge set into the oven door. This should be treated only as an indicator of the interior temperature on most old-model stoves. Even if the needle *is* in working order, invest in a hanging oven thermometer if your experience as a cook demands more accuracy. However, by trial and error and without cost you can learn to assess the oven temperature—provided the proper kinds of wood are used in the firebox—by putting your hand in the oven temporarily. This should indicate to you whether the oven is warm, hot, or very hot (which essentially is what both the oven-door thermometer and old cookbooks will tell you anyway). Another method is to lay scraps of white paper in the oven and to judge its temperature according to the amount of time the paper took to turn brown and scorch. There are no written directions for this kind of experience.

From the stories of feasts in the days before electricity, there seems nothing that a wood stove oven cannot do, although it takes more careful watching than modern ovens with automatic controls. Bread should be baked in a hot oven that is allowed to cool by shutting down the front damper, the chimney damper, and cracking open the check. To assure evenness (the firebox wall of the oven is the hottest side), the loaf pans should be watched and turned occasionally. If the top crust starts to brown too quickly, lay a piece of brown paper bag over the loaf. Even a soufflé—although a product of France originally and probably cooked in the more steady heat of a coal fire—can be attempted in a wood stove oven, provided the trick of maintaining a steady temperature through the selection of wood and manipulation of the dampers is learned.

Another way of using the potential of your wood stove is to take advantage of the firebox. When the wood has burned down to coals, chop them up with a poker and level the bed. Then throw on a steak or lamb chops. Sear them on both sides and cook quickly. If apple wood has been used for the fire, the results will satisfy the most discriminating taste.

Old-fashioned baked beans—costly for the modern electric stove cook—can be prepared economically in a wood stove. Leave the pot in the oven, heated by a steady-burning red oak log, and let it fend for itself all day with an occasional addition of liquid. By dinner time the beans will be ready. Meanwhile, on the stove top start soup simmering in a cast-iron pot. Add scraps of meat and vegetables from time to time for a nourishing and convenient *pot-au-feu* meal.

There are several important things to bear in mind if wood stove cooking is to be both worthwhile and enjoyable. Keep a neat and orderly wood pile where dry stove wood is available as needed. Clean out the ashpit and soot from around the oven frequently to reduce possible fire hazard and allow the dampers and stovepipe to function efficiently. Ashes should be kept in metal buckets or ashcans at a safe distance from the house, for wood coals have surprising longevity. If kept dry, these ashes can later be used for making lye—the first step in home soap production (see Chapter 26)—or spread on the garden to increase the potash content. Wood ashes are not much good for sprinkling on the icy walk in winter; they find their way back into the house too quickly!

Three more points should be mentioned to increase the enjoyment of using a wood cookstove. If your children are still young enough to be malleable, train them early to the onerous daily task of keeping the woodbox filled. This is a tedious but necessary process, and its neglect may result in a trip to the woodshed for a reason other than the gathering of wood.

Never use the oven as a storage closet for dirty dishes when unexpected company knocks, or for hiding valuables if you should leave the house. Human memory may not warn you to look in the oven before lighting the next fire.

Finally, if the results of cooking are to benefit both the family and the cook, clearly establish a basic rule: *only the cook* regulates the dampers while a meal is being prepared. Many a dish has been ruined and many a temper roused by a seemingly innocent fiddling with the drafts when the cook's back is turned. The best place for the noncook—and one of the most enviable in the house—is in the rocking chair next to the stove where one can be near enough to be warm and appreciative but not get in the way.

REFERENCE

Havens, David, "The Woodburners Handbook," Media House, Box 1770, Portland, Me. 04104

Digging and Stoning a Well

Stonemasonry is a dying art. So is well digging. To find a capable countryman who can both dig a well and stone it up is nearly a fruitless quest. Labor costs and newer methods of finding water have limited the appeal of this ancient profession.

But the homesteader—as interested today as he ever was in locating a dependable source of water for his house and barns—can dig and stone his own shallow well if he labors for love and experience. And if he lives in hilly country, he can also pipe the water to the house by gravity and keep both costs and maintenance to a minimum.

The first settlers were drawn to natural springs. These were later enlarged and stoned and sheltered to keep perishable foods longer and to provide a haven of coolness on a sultry summer's day.

It is possible to resurrect a dug well of proven ability. Or the homesteader can dig and stone one himself. Drilling wells is less risky today than it was even twenty years ago because of advances in technique and equipment, but it is still a gamble and often an expensive business. While it is true that shallow dug wells may dry out in extended periods of drought, they will provide an energyless source of water when operating.

Shallow wells are cylindrical holes usually about 3 feet in diameter and from 4 to 25 feet deep. Anything beyond this depth is termed a deep well; anything more than double the diameter is often called a cistern or reservoir. Although dug wells may be over 80 feet, these are rare.

Many shallow wells that were constructed two hundred years ago here in New England are still in operation, although with the increase in water consumption by the average American family (estimated at three hundred and fifty gallons per day), they are often used to supplement a drilled well or as a standby source in case of power failure. Many are in their original shape, which attests to the art of the builder; others have been lined with protective sleeves or further deepened to increase the supply. Some were abandoned. They were either filled in with stone to prevent misfortune, or left planked over—a potentially dangerous practice as the plank cover rotted away.

Originally the dug well was covered with removable boards, which allowed the water boy to sink his bucket and haul it up hand over hand or on a simple winch. Later the well sweep gained acceptance as a labor saver. Finally the pitcher pump was invented and mounted on planks or through a hole in a granite well stone, and the art of priming the pump and maintaining suction became progress. (The corollary art of challenging a little brother to put his tongue on a frosty pump handle was also developed about that time.)

One man who has considerable experience with dug wells is George A. Wood of Westminster, Vermont. According to a colleague, the retired Mr. Wood was never so happy as when diddling around in the bottom of a well—whether 8 or 80 feet down. He gained worldwide fame in 1967 on Valentine's Day when he was buried for six-and-and-half hours in a 12-foot well that collapsed while being repaired. That February day, several concrete tile insertions slipped when Mr. Wood was installing them to shore up the sides of the well.

When Mr. Wood's helper shouted down that he was going for

help, the veteran well digger is said to have called up, "Guess I'll be here when you get back."

A further cave-in buried him completely before help (in the form of a crane, three backhoes, an emergency rescue squad from Brattleboro, and television cameras) could get to him. For five hours he breathed through scuba diving hoses connected to oxygen tanks.

Digging or repairing a well can be dangerous, but not many homesteaders are going to dig too deeply. Most home wells in the country are from 6 to 15 feet deep. Once dug and stoned, a well should last practically indefinitely unless there is a marked change in the water table.

There are many bits of folklore and superstition to be investigated before starting to dig a well. One of these is dowsing, or water witching. Mr. Wood has no faith in dowsers—or rather, he has more faith in his own ability to judge from experience geologic formations, plant life, and the general lay of the land for aid in locating a projected well. He has pockmarked a considerable area on both sides of the Connecticut River valley with wells, never using a water witch.

There are those who claim dowsing is a gift possessed by only one in seven people. A research scientist recently announced that the art of finding water with a willow fork is connected with body chemistry and a peculiar alignment of neutrons and protons inherent in the makeup of the dowser.

Despite the long-standing New England veneration of dowsing, Mr. Wood disdains it and has dug wells enough in his lifetime to prove that water can be found without it.

Once the site for a well has been selected, the homesteader can hire a backhoe, which will dig down to 13 or 14 feet, or he can do the job laboriously with pick and shovel and buckets. A shallow well 3 feet in diameter will require an original excavation of more than twice that width. To dig a hole only 4 feet in diameter will hinder the digger; he needs all the space he can get to maneuver in.

Dug wells must penetrate to the ground-water table if they are to be sustaining. The water table generally follows the contours of the land and is higher under hills than beneath valleys. It may rise or drop during rainy spells and drought conditions. The bottom of the well must reach into the area of saturation.

Ground water travels for many miles. All water is constantly seeking its way to the sea, where it is drawn up again into the clouds to fall back on the earth in an endless cycle. Unless obvious sources of pollution are nearby (septic systems, livestock, open sewage, etc.), water will be purified as it moves through the earth. However, some water-borne diseases can travel for miles; others are attributable to faulty well construction, particularly where surface water penetrates the well. Some builders maintain that stones used in well construction must never have been exposed to air as in that case they would already harbor forms of pollution.

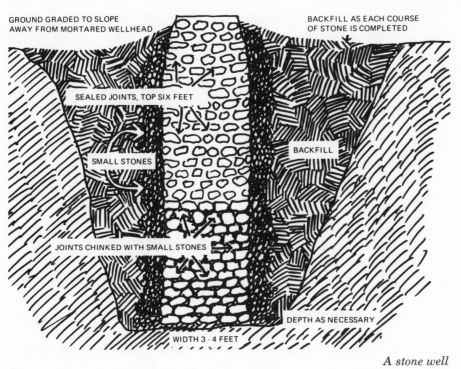

GROUND GRADED TO SLOPE
AWAY FROM MORTARED WELLHEAD

BACKFILL AS EACH COURSE
OF STONE IS COMPLETED

SEALED JOINTS, TOP SIX FEET

SMALL STONES

BACKFILL

JOINTS CHINKED WITH SMALL STONES

DEPTH AS NECESSARY

WIDTH 3 - 4 FEET

A stone well

All of this means that well water must be tested before it can be used for drinking. This can be done through your State Board of Health. Follow the directions for collecting water samples. The ensuing report will show with what chemicals and bacteria you have to contend. It will also recommend what to do to correct chemical imbalances, if possible.

Stoning a well is done without mortar. After the excavation has been made and a steady supply of water located, stones are laid in a circular pattern 3 to 4 feet in diameter. When a full circle is completed and chinked with smaller stones, the spaces outside the ring are filled with more stone to hold the well lining and provide an additional reservoir. Thus each circle is laid, chinked, and back filled. Mortar at this point would "seal" the source and increase the lime content in the well water.

The home well digger should consider the projected height of the well and estimate the amount of stonework necessary to complete the job. A shortcut can be taken by investing in a steel culvert. This is held vertically by embedding stones and gravel around it and tamping in excavation dirt as the work progresses upward. Or one could buy concrete well rings (3 feet in diameter, 2 feet high) and install them as he goes. Some well diggers prefer the latter, fearing that metal will eventually taint the water and increase the iron content.

No matter how deep the dug well, it must be protected from surface contamination. The upper 6 feet of the well casing must be sealed on the outside with watertight cement grout (or good clay) and the exposed part of the well shaft mortared. The top should be capped with a manhole cover or cement lid. Dirt can be mounded around the well head and sloped away from it, or trenches dug to prevent surface runoff from penetrating the shaft.

Removing the dirt while digging the shaft is a hard enough job. This can be done by the bucketload or by rigging up cables and pulleys to ease the load when the going gets deeper. Getting rid of the water is even more of a challenge once it starts seeping into the well side. A hose can often siphon the water off if the well is on a hillside. Otherwise, a gasoline-operated pump will be necessary if bailing out the well by buckets will not do the job fast enough. (One precaution *must* be taken when using an engine, however. Be sure to locate it as far from the well as possible to prevent the exhaust from entering the hole where you are working.)

To set up a gravity-feed water system (see illustration), the well should be located at a level at least 50 feet higher than the house—the higher the better. One-half pound of pressure is assured for each foot of drop. Twenty-five pounds can be had with this minimum elevation. The delivery pipe must be buried below frost line in as straight and gradually sloping a line as possible. A standpipe should be located in the well to allow accumulating air bubbles to escape or one may be tapped into the delivery line. A ram will be needed to boost the water from the well to a storage tank if the flow cannot be maintained otherwise.* The well outlet pipe should be

---

* *A hydraulic ram was once a common device. This helped to increase the velocity of the water by incorporating an air chamber and two valves between the source pipe and the drive pipe. For more information about rams, write: The Rife Hydraulic Engine Manufacturing Co., Box 367, Millburn, N.J. 07041.*

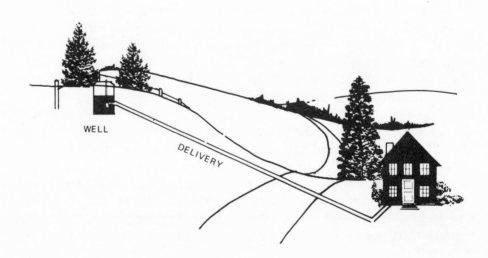

WELL

DELIVERY

A gravity-feed water system. The water source should be located at least fifty feet above the house to assure sufficient water pressure.

covered with a strainer and located a foot above the floor of the well to prevent sand and dirt from entering the system.

While many authorities recommend lining the well floor with pea stone, Mr. Wood is opposed. He suggests that any jagged surface such as crushed gravel will encourage snails and other forms of aquatic life to breed. (If one does find snails abundant in his well, he should dig down 2 feet around the well head, sprinkle a 70 percent chlorine solution in the trench, then pack good clay in the stone crevices before refilling the trench and grading the earth.)

Another country custom is to put a fish in the well to devour insects. If the well is properly sealed, Mr. Wood contends that you will not have enough insects to bother about. You *will* have a dead fish to scoop out. There are many kinds of pollution to contend with; no need to add obvious ones.

Few old-time stone wells need repair except in the upper several feet, which should be checked and remortared periodically to

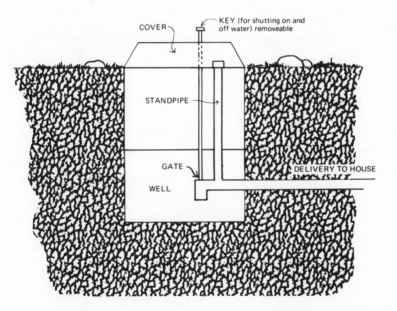

Arrangement of pipes in well.

prevent surface water and wildlife from entering. If, however, a dependable well shows signs of deterioration, it can be shored up by telescoping round sections of steel tile in the shaft. The top section, for example, might be 4 feet in diameter. This is inserted in the well to a stopping place. Another collar 3½ feet in diameter is lowered inside and below the first, etc. Finally all sections are grouted to prevent seepage.

Ancient dug wells may be encouraged to produce more water by driving a specially constructed head with a perforated section below the well floor. This is pounded with mallets or weights and sections of pipe added until the water supply is markedly increased.

Although accustomed to working underground in cramped quarters with constant exposure to all kinds of possible danger, Mr. Wood remains remarkably calm. In his opinion the greatest drawback to his career in well digging and repairing is not the danger—which he tends to minimize—but the stench of a dead and disintegrating snake, which from time to time he has been summoned to bucket out from someone's well. It's worse than a woodchuck or a skunk, he claims, and certainly far worse than being buried alive and living to tell about it.

REFERENCES

Farmers' Bulletin 2237 USDA: "Water Supply Sources for the Farmstead and Rural Home" (Available from the U.S. Government Printing Office, Washington, D.C. 20402—price 15¢).

Kains, M. G., "Five Acres and Independence," Pocket Books, New York, 1948.

How to Build a Smokehouse

Smoking meat is usually a midwinter chore, but summer is the time to plan your smokehouse, while the weather still holds and your pig is gaining weight. It can be a simple, open-ended barrel, a permanent stone or cement-block outbuilding, or any number of variations in between.

Smoking heightens the flavor and color of pork. It also helps seal the pores to guard against deterioration by mold and insects, solidifies the meat for long-term storage, and increases its keeping power.

The earliest settlers smoked their meats under primitive conditions. Once they were established, they incorporated a smoke hole in the chimney construction of their houses. This was a bricked or stoned closet—with access from the back side of the chimney or from the second floor—through which smoke passed on its way up the flue. Meat was suspended from hooks and direct heat from the fireplace was deflected. Too much heat during the smoking process is detrimental to the finished product; high temperatures will cook the fat and allow smoke to penetrate too quickly, making the meat strong-tasting and stringy.

If your house is not equipped with a smoke hole—or if to use it would be hazardous—you can build a makeshift barrel smokehouse outdoors, make a portable wooden shelter that can be stored away, or construct a permanent building.

The easiest arrangement to set up is the barrel. Some countrymen merely knocked out both ends of a wooden barrel, set a smudge

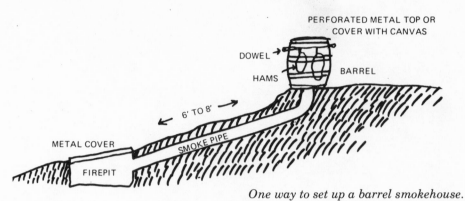

One way to set up a barrel smokehouse.

of corncobs within it on the ground, suspended their hams and flitches of bacon from dowels at the barrel head, and covered it all with canvas or other heavy material to keep the smoke from leaking. The disadvantages of this method are that only a little meat can be smoked at one time, and it is inconvenient to keep the smudge going continuously.

A more permanent barrel method is to bury a 6-inch-diameter ceramic tile pipe sloping upward from a fire pit to the smoking barrel. This pipe should be 6 to 8 feet long. Composition sewage pipes will not stand up to the heat and therefore tend to burn should your smudge get too hot. The resulting odor of creosote will permeate your hams and bacon and thereby ruin them. The ceramic tile pipe will conduct the smoke but discourage too much heat. The fire pit cover, which helps regulate the draft, must be metal to prevent it from charring or burning through. A metal disk can be suspended above the pipe where it enters the barrel to spread the smoke and prevent drippings from running down the pipe. Meat is hung from dowels in the barrel head.

For those who have both room for storage and a larger amount of meat to smoke, the portable wooden smokehouse is an easily built structure. Tongue-and-groove boards are used to prevent leakage. Because the building is held together with only eight screws, the sides and roof can be knocked apart and put away for another year. The fire is made in a metal bucket at the bottom of the smokehouse and can be tended by reaching through the lower door. For safety, the fire pot should be set on cleared ground or on a large flat stone. Meat can be hung from movable 2″ x 2″ rafters and checked by opening the upper door. Air vents in the gable ends of the building regulate the draft and passage of smoke.

By far the most permanent smokehouse is the kind built and operated by Charles Fox of Canterbury, New Hampshire. This is a mortared fieldstone outbuilding about 7′ x 9′ with a cement floor, drain, and detached fire pit. The eaves are 8 feet from the ground. Smoke vents in the gable can be opened and closed.

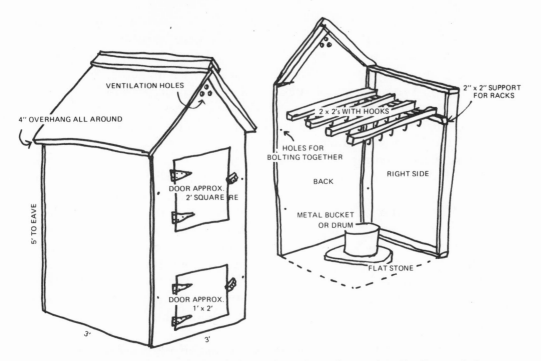

ABOVE. *Portable wooden smokehouse, bolted together and easily dismantled.*
BELOW: *A well-constructed permanent smokehouse.*

Fox is now a custom curer and smoker, licensed by the state, but when he built his smokehouse he was only interested in home production. Soon he was smoking hams for his neighbors. During eight months of commercial smoking—with additions to and changes in the original structure—Fox has processed eight hundred pigs. Most of them were brought, dressed, to his farm home.

The fire pit is located on the north side of the building and slightly lower, to allow smoke to enter through the smokehouse floor. (This is being changed, as Fox found that north winds in winter hindered fire-tending. The new fire pit will be on the opposite side.)

The smokehouse took all of one summer to construct. Piles of stone were brought in before building began. A standard cement-sand mix of 1 to 4 was used. The first step was to erect forms to contain the stones as the walls went up, but these were soon discarded to allow Fox and his family to see the results of what they were doing. Walls went up by eye, and work was slow. Fox tried to find stones that had at least two flat sides, a challenge even though his property abounds in stone walls.

Originally the interior was sheathed in plywood, but this was replaced by asbestos to comply with state regulations when Fox was granted a commercial license.

Fox uses red oak to smoke his bacons and hams. Traditionally, hickory is associated with smoked meats. "There isn't enough hickory in this area," he says. "Old-timers around here used red oak. It takes two years to dry, so if you use it the first year, you get more smoke than fire."

He pulled open the fire-pit door to show a couple of slightly glowing, split logs. "You don't need much wood," he explained, "to get the right amount of smoke."

Fox uses only corncobs to get the fire started. As with every art, each practitioner has his own methods and often disagrees with all the other experts. Apple wood and hard maple are other commonly used woods. Resinous woods must be avoided; they will taint the flavor. Wood used when green will produce more smoke than heat. If the fire burns too hot, throw on some hardwood sawdust to dampen it. Should you start your fire with pine, be sure the twigs or chips have burned out completely or have been removed before shutting the smokehouse door.

Cured meat absorbs smoke slowly, so do not fill the smokehouse with a thick cloud. It is better to let the smoke trickle among the hanging, separated cuts. Otherwise it can discolor rather than permeate the meat.

Some practitioners smoke continuously for two days; others start a smudge whenever they happen to be going by. This might take several weeks to achieve the proper color and flavor. Charles Fox smokes his hams four days continuously, keeping constant watch over the temperature.

DAVID ASGARD

If protected from insects and animals, smoked meat can be left hanging in a smokehouse that does not get too hot in late summer.

For home production, your taste and schedule will determine the method to follow. Some must have their hams mahogany-color before they consider them processed.

Smoked meat can be left hanging in the smokehouse (provided it is safeguarded against insects and animals) if the building does not get too hot later in the summer. The meat can be brought into the kitchen when needed. Otherwise, it should be hung in a well-ventilated, dry, dark place. Some wrap their hams in cheesecloth and paper before hanging. Mr. Fox suggests storing hams in loose-fitting plastic bags in the bottom of which is a crumpled sheet of newspaper to catch the drippings. The covering must be loose to allow air circulation, which discourages mold.

Smoking meat for home use need not be a rigorous occupation and is certainly not harassed by regulations. Because pork is the meat most commonly smoked on the farm, care should be taken to follow assiduously each step in the butchering, curing (see p. 163), and smoking processes. Pork spoils quickly if allowed to remain too long under unfavorable conditions.

With so few meat processors left in the country, building and operating your own smokehouse may lead you to experiment with different kinds of meat and cheeses you had not thought possible to preserve at home.

REFERENCE

Wigginton, Eliot, ed., *The Foxfire Book,* Anchor Books, Doubleday and Co., Inc., New York, 1972, pp. 199–201.

Constructing an Apple-Picking Ladder

My long two-pointed ladder's sticking through a tree
Toward heaven still, . . .

—ROBERT FROST

If your woodlot contains a variety of trees in different stages of growth and you have time to go beyond cutting cordwood this winter, there are many simple wooden products you can make to use around the farm and homestead. One of the most necessary is a ladder that will be light enough to carry around and yet durable enough to last for years.

There are craftsmen upcountry who supply dozens of ladders to professional apple pickers each year, but even if you are a rank beginner who can use hand tools, you can make a ladder from your own woodlot. Given certain basic tools on hand—a ripsaw, maul and wedges, mallet, drawknife or plane, hammer, pipe clamp, and brace with two different sized bits—the only purchase you will have to make is a handful of 1½ inch (4d) finishing nails.

Once your wood has been selected, cut, dried, and shaped to specifications, it should take about an hour to assemble a safe, good-looking ladder.

Plan ahead to have the wood ready to use. Red oak makes good rungs. It is strong and durable yet can be worked while still green. It is easier to split and shave than white oak. For the rails use spruce or ash. These woods are relatively free from knots (which weaken a ladder), yet are light enough to carry in ladder form.

Select a tree for the rails from a thick stand in your woodlot. This will assure good, straight growth. To make a standard 18-foot apple-picking ladder (for which you will find many other uses), choose a tree that is about 4 inches in diameter at a height several feet off the ground. When you have felled it (cut to slightly more than your finished length) and brought it home, peel off the bark and trim all branches flush to the trunk with an ax.

The pole is now ready for you to rip it in half lengthwise and start the drying process. You can either rip tediously with a hand ripsaw or use a chain saw or bench saw. The last two of course will do the job much more quickly, but you will need plenty of room to maneuver and a helper to guide the saw. In colonial times, pit saws were used—one sawyer located on the superstructure above the log, and the other in the pit below.

Spruce may twist and warp while drying so you will have to restrain it for from six to nine weeks depending on the weather. Construct four uprights about 4 feet apart. Across each, nail a pair of braces not more than 2 feet long. Leave room between each pair to insert your halved rails (flat side down) and a wooden wedge to prevent twisting (see diagram).

Professional ladder makers often cut their stock in late spring after the garden has been planted if they plan to complete the assembly in time for apple picking. However, harvesting the rails is something you can do at any time of year when work is slack.

Oak for the rungs will take longer than the rails to air dry, but you should work it into shape while still green because it will be easier to split when freshly cut. After you have felled your tree, saw several sections of the log into chunks 2 feet long. Now split these

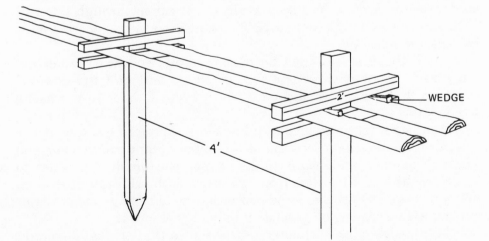

If the wood chosen for the rails has a tendency to twist while drying, restrain it in this manner for six to nine weeks.

with your maul and wedges, quarter them, and reduce in size to 2″ x 2″ squares, 2 feet long.

A standard 18-foot ladder will require seventeen graduated rungs, each decreasing ½ inch from a maximum length of 22 inches over all for the lowest rung. With a 4-inch tree, the inside measurement at the butt of the finished ladder will be about 18 inches. Dowel both ends of each rung to fit holes bored in the side rails. The first eleven rungs should be doweled to fit ¾-inch holes; the top six should be shaped to fit ⅝-inch holes. This helps prevent the upper reaches of the ladder rails from splitting.

The rungs themselves can be left roughly shaped for better purchase, or you may want to round them to avoid splinters while using the ladder. This can be done after the ladder has been assembled.

Use a lathe to dowel the ends of the rungs or clamp each in a bench vise and round them with a drawknife.

When your material has been properly cured, you are ready for the final step before assembling your ladder. Lay the pair of dry rails on the ground, making sure the butts are aligned. Mark off 1-foot intervals beginning from the bottom, and with brace and bit bore ¾-inch holes, centered in the rails, to receive the first eleven rungs. Change to a ⅝-inch bit and bore the remaining six pairs of holes at the top of the ladder rails.

Now you are ready to assemble your woodlot product. Lay out your rungs in order of decreasing length, the longest at the base of the rails and the shortest at the top. Set the rungs in one rail, flat side up.

Tap with a mallet or hammer until the rungs are properly seated in the holes. When you have completed one rail, place its mate on the upright rungs and align it from the bottom to the top of the ladder. Once each rung has been seated at both ends, lay the ladder on the ground and secure all of the rungs through one rail with 1½-inch (4d) finishing nails. This will keep the taper from pulling apart during use.

After the first rail has been completely nailed, draw in the other rail tightly with a pipe vise or clamp and nail the doweled rungs in it. All nails should be set to prevent danger to the user's hands later.

Another safety measure to take before completing the ladder is to saw off any excess tenons and drawknife or plane rough spots and knots. You may even want to sandpaper the finished product to guarantee the user freedom from splinters as the rails guide him up and down the ladder. The wood can either be left to age naturally or rubbed with a coating of linseed oil to help preserve it.

Many apple-picking ladders are made so that the rails meet at the top to allow easier penetration of the upmost branches of the tree. However, if your ladder is to be used for several purposes

When assembling the ladder, tap the rungs in one rail, flat side up, then place the last rail on the upright rungs and align from bottom to top.

After the first rail has been completely railed, draw in the other rail tightly with either a pipe vise or clamp and nail the rungs into it.

To prevent possible accidents or injuries to the user's hands, set all the nails, and saw off any excess tenons before the ladder is completed.

Once assembled, the ladder may be left to age naturally or rubbed with a coating of linseed oil to preserve the wood.

around the farm in addition to harvesting apples—gutter cleaning, shingling, house scraping and painting—the tapered construction described will provide more stability than the triangular kind as you lean the top against a flat, ungiving surface.

Ladders made by expert craftsmen for professional apple pickers receive hard, seasonal use. Their life expectancy is between five and seven years. However, the one you make and take care to keep dry should last nearly as long as you do.

Making Wattle and Other Portable Fences

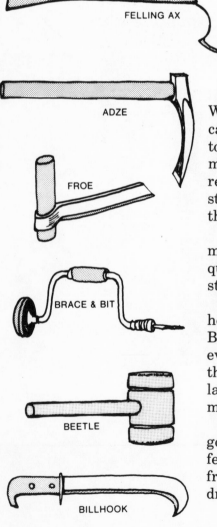

FELLING AX

ADZE

FROE

BRACE & BIT

BEETLE

BILLHOOK

When man first domesticated animals for his own use, he automatically created a problem—how to keep them in their place. And on today's homestead, good fences are a major but necessary investment, if one wants to keep his livestock safe and maintain good relations with his neighbors. As the costs of barbed wire, woven stock fencing, and electricity soar, more countrymen are turning to their own woodlots to help solve the fencing problem.

One way of confining and segregating small stock is to build movable sections of fencing that can be set up and rearranged quickly. When not in use, these portable wooden fences can be stored under cover, thus extending their useful life for years.

It would be futile to try to confine large animals—cows or horses, or even barnyard fowl—with portable, lightweight fences. But small stock—geese and turkey poults, replacement poultry and even orphaned lambs—can be controlled with a portable fence as the need arises. Sections can also be used for aged sheep during lambing, to divide the flock at breeding time, or for individual treatment such as shearing and worming.

The wattle fence was developed centuries ago and has undergone few changes. It can be built in 6- to 8-foot sections with only a few basic hand tools: the ax and billhook for cutting stock; the adze, froe and beetle for splitting and shaping; and the brace and bit for drilling holes.

Wattle is an ancient word that means to weave or plat. Thus

Portable wattle fences were used by our earliest settlers.

this kind of fence is made by weaving flexible branches (rods) or cleaved stock in and out among stronger uprights. The dimension of the rods will determine whether or not they should be split. If they are too thick to bend comfortably, you will have to split them lengthwise.

Materials for making a wattle fence can come either from a well-managed woodlot or from gleanings of second growth at the edges of meadows and shrubs from marshy areas.

Wattles should be made in uniform sections that are sturdy but easily handled. Traditionally the material was cut, sorted, and stacked to dry during the winter when the sap was down. Then the sections were assembled in the summer, right in the woods where the supplies had been left.

It takes very little time to make a section once you have prepared a fence form—this speeds the job and assures uniformity of each length. As the diagram shows, the form should be a slightly curved 8-foot log, split (see illustration a.). Lay the flat side on the ground and bore ten holes through the form about 1½ inches in diameter and spaced equally along the length of the log. The curve is important because when the section is removed from the form and laid on the ground in a stack, the weight of the other sections will straighten the curve, thus tightening the weaving and making a more durable fence. If a properly curved log cannot be found, use a plank 12 inches wide and 6 to 8 feet long. Mark it with a gentle curve along which you bore your holes with the brace and bit.

English crofters depended on ash saplings or split ash for the uprights (staves) and hazel for the rods. In this country hazel grows in shrublike thickets, and is hard to identify in the winter woods. In the late summer hazelnuts are a good identifying mark if you can get to them before the squirrels do. But other materials are suitable: ash and cedar for the staves; willow, hop hornbeam or ironwood, and even wild grapevines for the rods. The primary requirement of this kind of fence is that it be portable, so all materials should be as lightweight as possible. Split oak, for example, although notably strong, makes a fence that is too heavy to move comfortably.

The best-looking wattle fences are made from split stock. These sections have no loose ends sticking out to mar their appearance. However, if the homesteader needs a fence in a hurry, any flexible rod that can be bent without breaking will do. Vines and shrubs can be trimmed after the fence is built and will confine stock whether or not they look tailored.

Take your tools and your fence form to the source of supply to build your wattle fence. Set the form flat on the ground, but leave enough space around it to make weaving the rods easy. Select staves that are slightly smaller in diameter than holes that you bored in the form. Set the staves upright—heads down—in the form, taking care that the end staves are stouter and longer (about 5 feet if you are building a fence 3½ feet high) than the rest, for later they will be tapered to a point and driven into the ground to anchor the section.

Once the staves have been set, you can begin weaving. As diagrams a. to d. show, you first "let in" a rod at the bottom of the first three or four staves, weaving it in and out. Bend it around the end stave with a half-turn or twist before weaving it back. This twist will help prevent the rod from breaking. As you reach the end of each rod, let in a fresh one, weave it in and out, bend it around the end stave with a twist, and continue until you have reached the proper height. This will be about 2½ feet for young poultry, turkeys, and geese; 3½ feet for lambs and sheep. As in loom weaving, the end staves may want to slant inward as you progress. To combat this, do not pull your rods too tight as you weave.

When the section is finished but still in the form, trim off all but the end staves just beyond the woven rods. Then lift the section off the form and lay it flat on the ground off to one side. Trim the tops of the staves as well, to where they were inserted in the form.

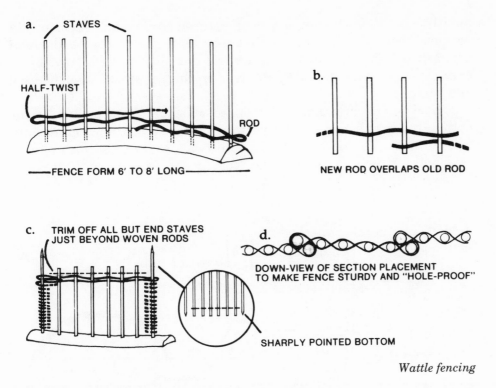

a. STAVES

HALF-TWIST

ROD

——FENCE FORM 6' TO 8' LONG——

b.

NEW ROD OVERLAPS OLD ROD

c. TRIM OFF ALL BUT END STAVES JUST BEYOND WOVEN RODS

d.

DOWN-VIEW OF SECTION PLACEMENT TO MAKE FENCE STURDY AND "HOLE-PROOF"

SHARPLY POINTED BOTTOM

Wattle fencing

The end staves should be sharply pointed at the bottom end about 1 foot below the wattle. As additional sections are finished, stack them one on top of another. This increasing weight will flatten the sections, thereby tightening them and making them more sturdy. (Professional wattle fence makers often leave a small part unwoven in the center of each section. This is done so that a pole can be inserted making it easier to carry several sections at a time.)

When enclosing an area with any kind of portable fencing, alternate the overlap of the sections as you pound them into the ground (see diagram d.). This gives the fence greater stability and eliminates the possibility of gaps between the sections.

Wattle fences can also be used as windbreaks, as a background for flower and vegetable gardens, to train pea vines, and—if made tall enough—for privacy.

Another type of homemade, portable fence is the hurdle. For this you should use split ash and you will need to learn to make mortise and tenon joints to fasten the ends of the horizontal bars into the upright staves.

The hurdle—still widely used today in rural England—is generally made in sections 8 to 10 feet long and 3½ feet high. Each section consists of two upright staves, six horizontal bars, and three cross braces.

To make a hurdle, split the ash stock with a froe and beetle, using the adze to widen the split as it progresses. These split lengths can be worked up green or stacked to dry. Ash splits easily because there are few knots that penetrate the trunk, and when dry, ash is light and resilient. The two upright staves are the posts of each section and should be made from thicker stock than the bars and braces.

Horizontal bars should be spaced wider at the top than at the bottom. This will thwart the natural curiosity of the confined animals. Mortise the ends of the bars into the staves. To do this, drill two holes which at their outermost measurement will be wide

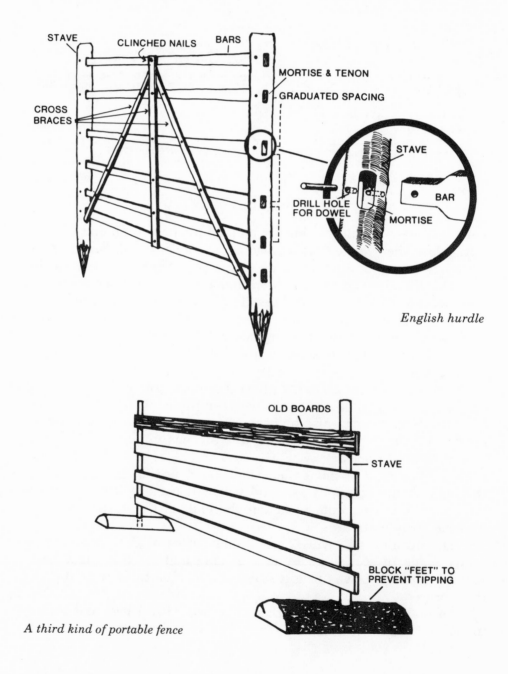

English hurdle

A third kind of portable fence

enough apart to accommodate the tenon of the bar snugly. Square off the mortise with a chisel and hammer. Then shape the tenon or tongue on the ends of the bars to fit the mortise. When all the bars have been inserted into the mortises, drill a hole through the staves and tenons for each joint, and hammer in a dowel to anchor them.

You will need three braces to strengthen the hurdle: one at the center point of the hurdle parallel to the staves; and two diagonal braces, which run from the top of the center brace to the bottom of the staves on each side of it. These braces can be held in place by hammering a nail through the braces and the bars where they cross. Use nails long enough so you can clinch them to keep them from pulling out.

Before you have finished each section, sharply point the bottom of the staves. As with the wattle sections, hurdles should be set up alternating the overlap of the sections to give additional strength to the portable fence.

There is a third type of movable fence, which resembles the hurdles trackmen use in races. However, these sections are not so easily moved and are of use mainly to sheepmen who want to control grazing. They are constructed of two uprights set into "feet"—heavy rectangles of wood, often split logs—like the bases of early Pilgrim harvest tables. The uprights are joined by boards or split stock nailed at graduated intervals. The finished sections will be heavier than either the wattle or hurdle fences. Usually, these are lined up end-to-end to section off parts of a larger fenced pasture.

Using raw materials around him, the homesteader can make portable fencing that will be used for many years, and help keep down at least one of the costs of keeping animals.

REFERENCES

Martin, George A., *Fences, Gates and Bridges—A Practical Manual* (original edition published in 1887), The Stephen Greene Press, Brattleboro, Vt., 1974.
Sloane, Eric, *A Museum of Early American Tools,* Ballantine Books, Inc., New York, 1964.
————, *A Reverence for Wood,* Ballantine Books, Inc., New York, 1965.

Making and Firing Durable Weatherproof Bricks

From the earliest times man has fashioned clay into regular shapes and sun-dried them to provide building material for adobe houses in regions where temperatures are high and no other suitable material—stone or wood—is available. But these sun-dried bricks will not hold up if exposed to northern winters. The manufacture of a durable, weatherproof brick requires that the sun-dried brick be fired in a kiln.

From April to October while the weather held, the manufacture of bricks on the homestead was a seasonal occupation of many New Englanders in the late eighteenth and early nineteenth centuries. These bricks were used to construct safer chimneys and more permanent buildings in a new land.

Colonial bricks—still found today in abandoned cellar holes—are thin, multicolored, irregular in dimension, and often warped. However, they are avidly sought for use in authentic restoration projects and command a handsome price, frequently as much as twenty-five cents a brick.

The ingredients necessary for brick-making haven't changed since ancient times: clay, sand, and water—all of which are still abundant in rural New England. If you wish to make your own bricks today, be prepared for hard work, and have on hand an ample supply of dry cordwood, cut into 4-foot lengths and split.

Beautiful colonial brickwork distinguishes the Richardson house in Bath, New Hampshire. Note the variations in color.

LAWRENCE F. WILLARD

Clay underlies much of New England, deposited in layers beneath the topsoil. Often areas of poor drainage indicate the presence of clay just below the surface, because the clay layer retards the percolation of water downward. Clay layers can also be seen as blue, gray, or yellow strata where the earth has been excavated, or along riverbanks.

To begin making bricks, dig an ample supply of clay and mix about 1 part of sand to every 2 parts of clay. According to David Goodrich, one of the great-grandsons of the founder of the W. S. Goodrich Brick Works in Epping, New Hampshire, sand controls shrinkage as the brick dries, and does not affect the porosity of the finished product. Be forewarned that unless it is mixed with other kinds of clay, New England's native blue clay produces a brick that is too dense, too brittle, and prone to shrinkage.

In the brickworks of the 1600s, clay, water, and sand were mixed until the ingredients flowed smoothly through a hole in the mixing form. Then it was allowed to settle, the water poured off, and the clay scored in the desired sizes—like marking off fudge in a mammoth pan—and left to dry. Finally, the bricks were fired.

Timothy Pickering, American Revolutionary War general and statesman, wrote to Noah Webster in 1792 and described the preliminary brick-making process of that period:

> Molds must be shod with iron, each mold made for a single brick. These are thrown into a tub of fine, sifted sand—not water—to prevent the bricks from sticking to the sides. To make 2000 bricks a day requires one molder, one man to work the clay, one man to wheel it to the tables, and a boy who bears off a single brick at a time.

Later it was found the composite molds were more efficient, even though they were heavier. These can be constructed of ⅝-inch stock to form six bricks at a time (see diagram page 55). The cross braces are rabbeted or dovetailed into the side rails, and the top and bottom edges of the perimeter are reinforced with iron strapping to prolong the useful life of the mold. Handles can be affixed to each end of the open mold to help the brick maker lift the form from newly made bricks.

Before you begin to construct your mold, determine the dimensions of the finished brick you want to work with. When clay dries and is fired, it will shrink overall by about ⅛ inch for each inch of original measurement (an 8-inch green brick, for example, will measure approximately 7 inches when finished. All its other original dimensions will be similarly reduced).

Although the dimensions of bricks manufactured today may vary according to the company that makes them and the tradition of the locality, as well as the specifications of the architect, modern-

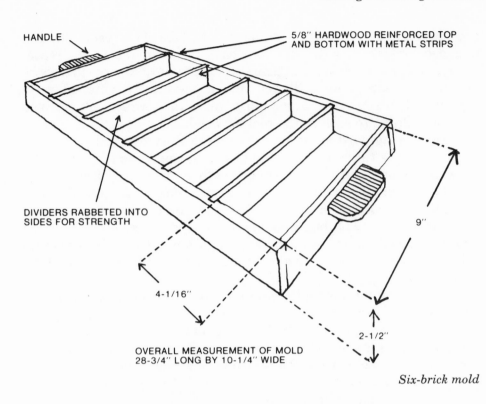

HANDLE

5/8" HARDWOOD REINFORCED TOP
AND BOTTOM WITH METAL STRIPS

DIVIDERS RABBETED INTO
SIDES FOR STRENGTH

9"

4-1/16"

2-1/2"

OVERALL MEASUREMENT OF MOLD
28-3/4" LONG BY 10-1/4" WIDE

Six-brick mold

day bricks are much more uniform than those made under the primitive conditions of colonial times. Most early brick measured approximately 1¾"×3½"×7". Today's finished brick is larger and more apt to be 2¼"×3½"×7⅝".

The molder lays the form on a tabletop or wooden pallet, presses the wet clay into each compartment, strikes it with a wet batten * to even the surface, and clears away any excess clay. He then lifts the mold by the handles so the green bricks are left, neatly spaced, on the pallet. Green bricks should be left in the mold only long enough to solidify partially (two to three minutes) or they will stick to the wooden sides. These fresh bricks are then carried either one at a time or by sixes on the pallet (a group of six will weigh about sixty pounds) to the drying yard.

If the mixture of clay, sand, and water is too soft for brick-making, add lime to give it body. If the mixture is too hard, add more water. The raw clay mixture should be about the consistency of jelly.

There are two kinds of brick that are made by the above process: sand-struck and water-struck. To make sand-struck brick follow the directions given by Pickering and dip the mold into a tray of fine sand before adding each new batch of clay. During the molding

---

* A flat narrow strip of wood longer than the mold is wide.

process some of the sand will adhere to the face of the brick and give it added texture; it will also help ease it out of the mold. Water-struck bricks are harder and present a more antique appearance. In this process the mold is dipped into a chemically softened water bath (Goodrich Co. uses water glass, an alkali), which acts as a lubricant, helping to release the molded brick.

The drying yard must be a level area fully exposed to the sun. Care should be taken in handling bricks in the green stage so as not to warp them. During hot, dry weather bricks should cure in twenty-four to forty-eight hours. They are "edged" frequently to encourage thorough, even drying. This periodic turning exposes each plane to the air. The brick maker is dependent on nature for this phase of the operation. A hard, pelting rain will ruin freshly molded bricks, but once they have solidified, rain will only retard the drying time.

By the late nineteenth century, most of the exposed drying yards were abandoned because of the brick maker's lack of control over the drying process. Racks were made to accommodate the wooden pallets on which the green bricks were molded, and the racks were protected from the weather by a roof. Today, commercial brick companies have completely enclosed drying areas and force-dry bricks with the exhausted heat from the kilns.

*Roofed drying rack
for green bricks.*

There are two kinds of brick kilns in general use today: the scove and the beehive. The former is a temporary oven constructed of the green bricks that are to be fired. When finished, the scove kiln is dismantled and the brick sorted and carted away. This is the most practical arrangement for the homesteader. The beehive kiln is used primarily by commercial brick makers and is a permanent oven made from specially molded and mortared bricks to form the domed sides and roof. The cavity of the oven is filled with green bricks; when these have been fired, they are removed and another batch is inserted for a future firing. The beehive kiln is usually constructed in anticipation of regular commercial production.

Once enough bricks have been dried in the yard or on racks at the homestead, you will be ready to construct a kiln. A homemade scove kiln can be built on a piece of level ground by simply stacking the dried brick from the ground up to form the bench and stepped-in arch of the kiln (see diagram). Be sure to leave plenty of space between the bricks, and make the arch wide enough to accommodate an ample firebox. The final length of the kiln will be determined by the number of bricks to be fired, but remember that it must be long enough to take the 4-foot lengths of cordwood. When the kiln has been completed, it should be "faced" with already fired brick stacked around the perimeter. This facing should then be smeared with a plasterlike mixture of sand, clay, and water, which will fill in holes on the outside of the kiln and help retain the heat. The daubing is retouched daily during the firing.

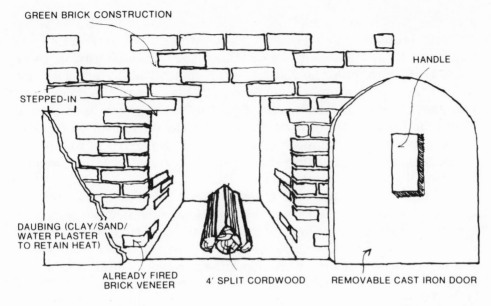

GREEN BRICK CONSTRUCTION

HANDLE

STEPPED-IN

DAUBING (CLAY/SAND/
WATER PLASTER
TO RETAIN HEAT)

ALREADY FIRED
BRICK VENEER

4' SPLIT CORDWOOD

REMOVABLE CAST IRON DOOR

The scove kiln

The scove kiln is an updraft furnace. One end of the arch is sealed with a cast-iron door, and wood is loaded into the other. When the fire is burning, the other end of the arch is sealed. In large scove kilns (sometimes they are 40 feet wide and have twenty arches), the firewood is replenished alternately from either end of the arch to get an even burn. Usually pine slabs are used to give a hot fire during the day, while slower-burning oak and maple keep the fire going at night. Temperatures reach about 1850°F. The fire is maintained, night and day, for about two weeks. In this type of kiln the bricks at the bottom are exposed to the greatest heat and will burn darker—from "brick" red to black. The bricks at the top of the arch will be lighter in color and softer in density. The clays native to New England generally contain enough iron to cause them to burn a deep red without additional coloring. However, the position of the brick will affect the final coloration.

The scove kiln will glow a cherry red during the firing. An early written report from Saco, Maine, advises that it will take from two days to a week of constant burning to fire brick in a scove kiln. Goodrich Brick Works fires from ten days to two weeks and allows another week for cooling before dismantling the kiln and sorting the bricks. However, their kilns burn up to 700,000 bricks at a time.

The final result is reversed in a beehive kiln (redder bricks at the top of the stack, yellower bricks toward the bottom) because this permanent furnace uses the down-draft method. The heat that rises to the undersurface of the kiln (made from specially shaped burnt brick) is forced down and through a gutter, which runs under the kiln floor and is exhausted through a stack that may also serve an adjacent beehive. This method is used by the Densmore Brick Co., of Lebanon, New Hampshire, which has been manufacturing brick since 1817, although the rising cost of fuel oil and electricity has caused them to discontinue temporarily this part of their business. Densmore manufactured much of the brick that was used to construct the Dartmouth College campus in nearby Hanover.

Commercial brick makers have largely converted to fuel oil for firing their bricks, but they still agree that using wood in the final stages will give the finished brick a better color.

Noggins, pluggins, and clinkins were colonial names for the bricks that were farthest from the fire; these anemic orange or pale cream bricks were used for filler in the construction of houses and chimneys. The bench brick—those that flanked the firebox—were the most durable. These were sometimes overdone and glazed to a dark color or even burnt. In some brick bonding the burned "headers" (the ends of the brick) were alternated with the red "stretchers" (the long side) to create patterns.

Today people will occasionally pave walks and terraces with old used brick, only to find that after a winter of exposure some bricks disintegrate and have to be replaced. These are soft bricks and were never intended for outside use; apparently when they were fired the temperature was not high enough. These bricks should be saved for interior use—cellar construction, chimney and wall fillers.

Brickworks like Goodrich in Epping, New Hampshire—the sole survivor of nearly two dozen yards that manufactured bricks in that town alone—still make colonial-sized brick for reconstruction work. Presently Goodrich is supplying bricks for the restoration work in the Faneuil Hall area of Boston.

Numerous towns throughout the six-state area supported local brickworks. During the past century, however, many brickyards have closed because of decreasing interest in brick as a building material. Meanwhile, the modern homesteader can carry on a craft that is older than the nation by making brick in his own backyard.

REFERENCES

Randall, Peter, "W. S. Goodrich, Inc.," *New Hampshire Profiles,* Nov. 1969.
Rawson, Marion Nicholl, *Of the Earth Earthy,* E. P. Dutton & Co., 1937.
Thomas, Matthew, "Historical Epping, N.H.," *Raymond* (N.H.) *Times,* April 9, 1975.

Laying Out a Good Driveway

Today's countryman relies on his driveway as his lifeline to the outside world especially if his house is set back from a town road—whether paved or graveled. Since by law most New England towns prohibit the use of their equipment on privately owned property, a driveway is the homeowner's responsibility. He must either hire someone with the machinery to build and maintain his drive or do it himself.

Whether using a pick and shovel or engaging a multiton bulldozer, he will find the principles of good road construction have not changed appreciably since the days of the pharaohs when one reportedly used 100,000 slaves over a ten-year period to build a road before he could begin to erect his pyramid.

Fortunately, scientific knowledge has taught us considerably more about soil structure and its properties since then; construction equipment has displaced slaves and captured armies; the time to complete the job has been dramatically reduced.

But, the elements of sound construction are the same now as they were thousands of years ago: a firm base and a durable surface. Some variations, improvements, and new materials have been introduced over the years. The Romans, for example, discovered the technique of compacting different layers of construction material to form a firm roadbed. They also realized the importance of good drainage in keeping together a far-flung empire. They scooped up soil from the borders of the proposed bed to create ditches, tamped down the fill on a foundation, and established their throughways above the level of the surrounding ground. Thus, they initiated the raised—or "high"—way, evidence of which can still be found in rural England.

Later, both French and Scottish road builders found that by crowning or rounding the foundation layers of the roadbed they kept the road drier and therefore more passable.

For New Englanders this underlying construction and attention to drainage is especially important because excessive water accumulation coupled with the extremes of seasonal temperatures will tend to play havoc with any road.

Traditionally, Yankee farmers sometimes skirted the problem of impassable roads during long winters or muddy springs. Although most farmsteads were built adjacent to well-traveled routes, those that were set back to take advantage of a particular site were often provided with an alternate means of getting in and out. When the fair-weather lane was mired in mud or drifted with snow for weeks or months at a time, the farmer hitched up his team and took off across the fields in a sleigh.

Today, however, fewer and fewer homesteaders have this choice because of changed priorities, the press of time, or lifestyles that will support a car or truck but not the luxury of a team of horses.

Before laying out a good, all-weather driveway or reconditioning an old one, the homesteader should first study the site and try to anticipate some likely problems.

Some of these may be in having to bridge naturally wet areas, in channeling surface runoff water to where it can do the least harm to the road, and in regulating the pitch of the drive either by spreading it out evenly along the entire length or by introducing curves that will make navigation easier.

Straight drives are the easiest to build provided the slope is not too steep. However, compromises can often be made. These could involve saving particular trees or natural and manmade features such as rock outcroppings and stone walls. All planning and execution should focus on the construction of the most effective drive with the least disturbance to the natural features of the land.

To prevent washouts on steeply pitched roads—and to avoid having to dig in culverts—many countrymen resort to constructing waterbars or "thank-you-ma'ams," which are low barriers of built-up gravel about 1' wide and extending obliquely across the road from one shoulder to the other. They help to slow down the force of runoff water and divert it from the road surface. Some old roads up and over mountains boast as many as twenty-five of these waterbars over the length of their climb. Whereas they are effective both in controlling water and in slowing down traffic, they can be a hazard to the modern driver who is unaware of their existence.

Even if the homesteader is not going to do the actual work himself—and this may be decided by the length of the drive, time, and the amount of skill and equipment it will demand of him—he should determine where he wants his driveway, how well he can afford to construct it, and be able to communicate it to a contractor. Often, if his house is a new one, road work must be done coincidentally to excavating for the cellar.

After marking out the proposed drive, establishing a firm footing is the first step in the actual construction of it. In New England, this excavation must be dug deeper than it is farther south to help combat the freezing and thawing action of the ground in spring. The depth will depend on the terrain and underlying strata but generally should be to about 3 feet. A one-lane drive is about 9 feet wide. The subsoil will greatly affect the durability of the finished drive. Coarse-grained, sandy soils provide good drainage; fine-grained clay and dense, cohesive soils often yield unfavorable results. These latter interfere with proper drainage.

If digging out the roadbed to rid it of unfavorable soil, muck, or organic matter is too much of a problem for the homesteader with little equipment and a long drive to handle, it is best to hire a heavy equipment operator. Although initially expensive, the work will go quickly and well if the landowner is on hand to reinforce his wants.

Once excavation has been completed, it is time to plan for future drainage. Sometimes, when the road is to pass through a naturally wet area on somewhat level ground, it will call for installing a culvert. This will lead the water under the roadbed from one side to the other. It can either be the prefabricated, metal type used by highway departments or constructed of rocks, bricks, granite slabs, or reinforced concrete. Whatever the material, the culvert should be set higher at one end than the other—depending on where the

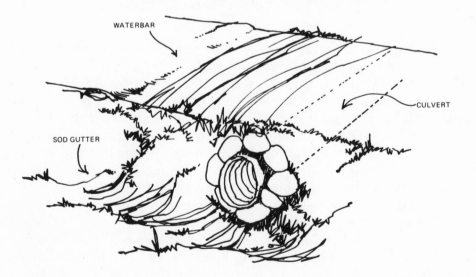

WATERBAR

SOD GUTTER

CULVERT

water is to go—and braced with large rocks to prevent shifting under the weight of passing cars. It should also be long enough to span the width of the driveway and protrude beyond the shoulders.

Most driveways are crowned unless the rise is gradual over a long distance. This encourages them to shed surface water. The sides of the finished road should rise at the rate of ½ inch from the shoulder to the center line for every 1 foot of surface distance.

To provide for this, a foundation layer of coarse stones—called *4 inch minus bank run* by local gravel contractors—can be dumped, spread, and crowned on the roadbed to a depth of about 2 feet. This is most easily done by a bulldozer or flat-bladed grader and followed up with some hand raking. On top of this add a 6 inch to 8 inch layer of 1½-inch crushed gravel. The best results will occur if this has been screened to eliminate particularly fine particles. Finally, spread a surface layer of ¾-inch crushed stone to a depth of 2 inches to 4 inches. Ideally, you should wet this down and roll it to keep it in place.

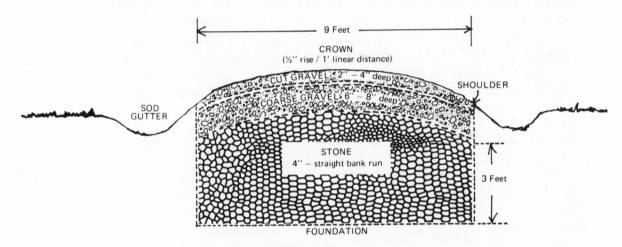

Sealing the driveway with asphalt or other nonporous material will certainly help to maintain the surface. When applied in semi-liquid form, this seeps through the fine layer of gravel and binds it together. Whether or not to pave your driveway will depend on several factors and a contractor will have to be retained for this kind of specialized job. One is expense. Another is in anticipating the normal use and weights your road will carry. A third is the surface condition of the town road your driveway joins. Many people living in the country choose to construct gravel rather than paved driveways because they believe there is more traction in freezing weather to encourage safe driving.

Another way to make a durable surface is to pave the driveway with stone blocks or brick. These, however, require hand labor for they do not lend themselves to mechanization and also require a tremendous amount of material. For an often equally durable sur-

face, you can spread and roll down a thin layer of breaker dust (a by-product of the gravel process) on top of the crushed stone. Concrete drives leading to a country farmhouse are rare sights.

Once your driveway has been built, further attention should be given to sloping the shoulders. This may require the construction of shallow sod ditches or gutters that parallel the drive and occasionally leave breaks that will cause water to fan out harmlessly in surrounding grassland or woods. Like the principle of the waterbars, these gutters are built to prevent running water—particularly in spring thaws and sudden downpours—from gaining momentum and eroding your drive. These, as well as the culverts, should be inspected periodically to prevent them from becoming clogged with debris (leaves, fallen branches, etc.), which will form natural dams and may feed the water back onto your drive. Sod gutters should be kept shallow enough so as not to encourage too fast a flow.

Even the best constructed driveways will have to be maintained. Aside from regular inspections, you may have to make sure no waterways form where you don't want them by filling in and raking gullies level. If your drive has been finished with finely crushed gravel, you will want to rake them back from the shoulders occasionally to where they will do more good. And finally, after years of wear, an additional load of gravel should be spread on the surface as part of a regular maintenance program.

Even if you are not faced with building a new driveway at this time, the knowledge of sound construction principles may help you to become a more effective citizen. You can station yourself on the shoulder of the unpaved town road that abuts your property every time the town equipment lumbers by and, remembering that this is your lifeline to the outside world, you are armed with knowledge. Leveling the crown, filling in drainage ditches, and breaking existing culverts with heavy machinery may help cover miles of back roads more quickly than the old-time labor force used to, but attention to these basic principles will in the long run save time, money, and frustration. While gentle criticism may not endear you to either your Road Agent or to the Selectmen, it will make more sense than to have a well-constructed private lane leading to a public bog.

Sharpening and Rehandling Hand Tools

Keeping knives and other common hand tools in prime cutting condition is the mark of a careful craftsman. Sharp tools make all jobs easier and faster. Whereas kitchen knives and woodworking tools demand constant attention throughout the year, the care given others—axes, hatchets, and garden tools such as spades, edgers, hoes, etc.—is more seasonal. Winter is a good time to plan for the gardening season.

With only a minimum investment in files or bench stones, many hand tools can be salvaged and reconditioned. Often these tools—if they have been handed down from father to son—are of better quality than similar ones manufactured today.

The homesteader is fortunate to have a wide choice of sharpening devices on the market, ranging from the simplest hand-held mill files and synthetic bench stones to the most expensive motor-driven grinding wheels. It is handy to have an electric grinder in your workshop because it will do the job more quickly, but most home sharpening can be done satisfactorily with less expensive equipment. Also, hand sharpeners have the added advantage of being portable.

When sharpening any tool there are several points to keep in mind: the original bevel (angle of the cutting edge) must be maintained, no more metal should be removed than is absolutely necessary to gain a sharp edge, and—if using an electric grindstone—the blade should be kept cool by dunking it in water frequently so as not to draw out the temper of the metal.

The bevel angle is formed by grinding away the sides of the blade to form a wedge, and this angle varies with each kind of hand tool. Often—with wood chisels, plane irons, scissors, hoes, etc.—the blade is beveled on one side only. Other tools such as knives and axes are beveled on both sides of their blades. The more acutely an edge is beveled, the more brittle it becomes. This means the edge will break down more frequently and have to be resharpened. Presumably—although you may purchase a new tool that is not as sharp as it should be—the manufacturer has ground the proper cutting angles for the job each tool will be expected to do.

The reason for not filing off more metal than necessary is twofold: too much grinding beyond that needed to establish a fine edge will reduce the life expectancy of the tool; and often, as with kitchen knives that are used regularly for precise work, the metal immediately behind the cutting edge is needed to support and strengthen it.

Before doing any sharpening, note the original angle of the cutting edge so you will be able to duplicate it—and at the same time look for any nicks in the blade. Since these will not cut, you should file or grind the blade beyond the deepest of these notches in order to establish a uniform, fine edge.

Microscopically, the sharpest blades are composed of a series of uneven, ragged planes. These allow the edge to take hold of the material being cut. A dull tool will feel smooth to the touch. Therefore, to test for sharpness—both before you begin and to tell you when to stop—feel the cutting edge with your thumb, applying only light pressure as you move it *across* the blade. If it catches at your skin, presumably it is sharp. A second method is to lightly shave the back of your hand with the blade. Finally, hold the cutting edge up to the light and squint along it as you gently rock it back and forth. A dull edge will reflect light and appear as a shiny, narrow surface, while a sharp edge will be invisible.

If you are hand-sharpening tools that are not particularly hard metal (axes, hatchets, garden hoes, shovels, etc.), buy a 10-inch bastard mill file. For finer work add a second-cut mill file and even a smooth mill file to your collection.

For harder metals that require even finer edges, there are hand and bench stones—both natural and synthetic—which will last a long time if cared for properly. These come in various grits from coarse to extra fine. You can also purchase a silicon carbide stone, which has a medium grit on one side and fine on the other. All stones should be used with a lubricant—a light household oil, mineral or kerosene, or as a last resort, water—which floats away metal

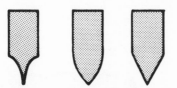

Different bevels produce different types of edges. LEFT: *concave bevel, hollow-ground edge.* CENTER: *convex bevel, cannel-ground edge.* RIGHT: *flat bevel.*

particles and prevents the pores of the stone from becoming clogged and ineffective. To clean a stone, place it in a pan and warm it in the oven or over a fire. Then wash it with gasoline or kerosene (not near an open flame!). Keep all sharpening stones covered when not in use to protect them from dirt and grime.

Other hand sharpeners include the traditional chef's steel or an abrasive cloth or paper tacked to a small wooden paddle. Hand- or foot-operated grindstones, which once graced the dooryards of most farms, can still be found at auctions and flea markets, but all too often the stones are so deteriorated that the grindstones are useless to the craftsman.

Modern professional bench grinders are driven by ½ hp motors. Be prepared to spend as much as $145 for a ball-bearing model with two stones and eye shields. Otherwise, salvage an unused home appliance electric motor from an old washing machine or dryer and convert it into a suitable bench grinder. You will be spending considerably less. If you have or intend to purchase a bench grinder, you might do well to investigate the new vitrified aluminum oxide grinding wheels. These man-made stones cut faster and cooler than the traditional carborundum grindstones, eliminating some of the danger of changing the temper of a cutting edge during the sharpening process.

Of course, there are combination can openers and grinders in most discount stores today. The knife-sharpener side is equipped with metal guides so you can re-create the original bevel of the blades.

If you prefer the ease and power of electricity but do not own any of these devices, you can buy an abrasive disc or mounted grinding wheel for your portable electric drill. However, the results of sharpening with a hand-held drill will be disappointing, for there is too much play while the grinder spins. More uniformly sharp edges can be obtained either by filing or grinding and then finishing off on a stone.

Here are some practical hints about sharpening a few of the more common hand tools.

(A) *Whetting a blade—the stroke is made with the cutting edge leading.* (B) *Stropping a blade—with the cutting edge trailing.*

KNIVES

Knife blades can be hollow-ground on a wheel. This produces a concave bevel with a radius equal to that of the wheel, and allows a finer cutting edge to be fashioned on a whetstone as a follow-up. If ground on the side of a wheel or on a bench stone, the bevel will be flat. Heavy-duty edges are shaped with convex bevels. The usual method of sharpening knives which are not badly nicked is to use a medium abrasive first and follow this with a fine grit oilstone. For the extra fine edge that you require on a boning knife, for example, strop the cutting edge on a piece of smooth leather.

Whetting a knife blade on an oilstone should be done with the cutting edge of the blade *leading* as you stroke elliptically across the stone. When stropping a blade, the cutting edge should be *trailing* the stroke.

Sharpening blades will often produce a jagged roll of thin metal along the cutting edge. This is called a feather edge, wire edge, or burr. If it cannot be seen, at least it can be felt when you pull the blade lightly across the back of your hand or a piece of fabric. This is one signal to stop sharpening because it means the edge is thin to the point of perfection. To remove the burr, whet the blade with the cutting edge trailing.

AXES AND HATCHETS

These seem particularly susceptible to nicking unless one is a superlative woodsman. Unlike chisels, they are angled on both sides of the blade. After grinding or filing away imperfections, whet the blade (in circular movements if using a hand stone, or in long strokes at an angle if using a file). The blade of a chopping ax should be filed somewhat thinner than one used for splitting wood.

GARDEN TOOLS

It is remarkable how much easier garden work can become with a sharpened hoe, spade, or edger. Insert the tool in a bench vise and file with long strokes across the upper side of the cutting edge. Hoes can also be sharpened on the sides of their blades as well, which will allow the gardener to nip off weeds in less accessible places. Touch-up filing can also be done on hedge clippers, pruning hooks, rotary lawn-mower blades (remember it is very important to keep the two sides of a rotary mower blade evenly balanced, to avoid excessive vibration when running), shovels and other hand tools used around the garden and fields.

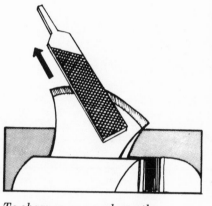

To sharpen an ax, clamp the head in a bench vise and file with a mill file in the direction and at the angle shown by the arrow.

REPAIRING AND REPLACING HANDLES

Too many serviceable tools are thrown away when their handles break. New handles can be shaped at home by the careful workman who knows the properties of wood, or replacement handles are readily available at lumber and hardware stores and can be made to fit all varieties of common tools.

To replace a broken or split handle, you must first remove it. Clamp the tool in a bench vise and with a hacksaw saw off the handle even with the head. Remove the remaining wood from the eye of the tool by first drilling a series of holes and then forcing the

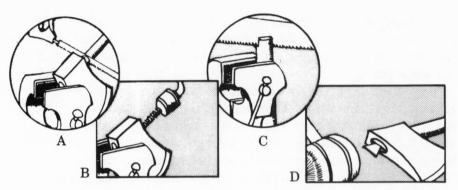

Rehandling an ax. (A) *Saw off old handle;* (B) *drill out the hole in the ax-head.* (C) *cut kerf, or slot in new handle;* (D) *insert new handle into head and pound wedge into the kerf. Lastly, saw off and handle even with ax-head.*

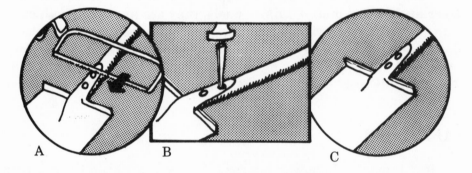

Rehandling a spade. (A) *Saw off rivet heads in old handle;* (B) *punch out rivets;* (C) *insert new handle. Then drill holes for rivets in new handle; insert rivets and hammer down the rivet heads.*

pieces out with a hammer and punch. Work the replacement handle down to a proper fit with a rasp, trying it in the eye of the tool frequently. If using a wooden wedge to fix the handle in place, be sure the kerf (a slit in the end of the handle) is cut so that it extends more than halfway down the head of the tool when the handle is in place. This is not necessary when using a metal wedge. Drive the new handle into place with a mallet by either striking the metal head or hitting the base of the handle. When the handle is properly seated, drive in the wedge. Saw off the protruding head of the handle so that it is flush with the top of the tool.

Most craftsmen recognize individual idiosyncrasies with regard to the proper angle one should maintain between the head and handle of such tools as axes and hammers. When you find a particular hammer, for instance, that feels especially comfortable to use—they are *not* all the same—make a pattern of the relationship between the head and handle. Should you ever break the handle, this pattern would be most useful. In the absence of any pattern, a general rule is that when the face of the hammerhead is resting on a flat surface, the end of the handle should just touch the surface as well.

Many shovel and spade handles are riveted. To replace these, the rivet heads must be ground or filed down and the rivets punched out. Remove the remainder of the broken wooden handle by drilling and punching, fit the replacement, and bore holes that will line up with those in the shovel shank. Insert the new handle and rivet it in place, using a ball-peen hammer.

Keeping tools sharp is a continuous process, and it is a necessary chore that can be perfected only by experience. But a really fine-edged tool will make any cutting job in woodlot or kitchen easier, quicker, and more pleasant.

REFERENCES

Jones, M. M., *Shopwork on the Farm,* McGraw-Hill Book Co., New York, 1945.
Walton, Harry, *Home and Workshop Guide to Sharpening,* Popular Science-Outdoor Life Books, distributed by Harper & Row, New York, 1967, Revised 1973.
Weygers, A. G. *The Making of Tools,* Van Nostrand Reinhold Co., New York, 1973.

Plant Life

Managing the Small Woodlot

Once the home woodlot stood like money in the bank. It was drawn upon for seasonal needs and sometimes depleted in times of emergency. Woodlot operation was an integral part of a system of interrelated activities on the New England family farm. Wood was taken from it to heat the home and cook meals; poles and posts fenced the pastures; lumber was there for beams, planks, boards and shingles, for home repair and new construction; sawlogs were sold to local mills for cash profit. Enough timber was left growing—hopefully—to allow the farmer's widow and children, if need arose, to carry on.

Today, as many professional foresters agree, the small woodlot owner, with holdings of from ten to fifty acres, is doing less and less in his woods each year. This lack of activity and interest is due to a change in lifestyle and a shift in personal priorities. Most heads of households earn their living away from home. With their salaries they can buy fuel and building supplies. For recreation many find it more exciting to snowmobile through the winter woods than to work in them.

It is also partly due to an environmental concern in which the injunction to "spare that tree"—voiced in the 1830s and intended to slow down the greedy lumber barons—is being taken literally.

A new generation of landowners has arrived, and many of them don't realize the possibilities their woodlots offer. They also don't know how to begin—or where.*

---

* NOTE: Before doing anything on property you think is yours, you should find out exactly *where* your boundaries are. We know of at least two cases where people have managed their neighbor's woodlot for a number of years before anybody discovered the mistake.

LAWRENCE F. WILLARD

What are some of the assets of a properly managed woodlot? The most obvious, perhaps, are lumber and cordwood. But there are by-products worth considering: sap for maple syrup and sugar; edible wild plants, fruits, and nuts; material for landscaping; provision of windbreaks, Christmas trees, and privacy; areas for camping and wildlife sanctuaries; trails for hiking, horseback riding, cross-country skiing, learning—or just plain loafing.

Ben Rice—the man who for a quarter of a century has written the country essays facing the calendar pages in *The Old Farmer's Almanac*—has given a lot of thought and energy to his family woodlot and has also voiced concern about the future use of forests in general. He and his wife own property, which has been in the family since 1896. Their ownership, he says, is not without restrictions and considerations and judgments not necessarily their own.

Since 1938, when the Rices bought the land from his father, they have been carrying on good silviculture practices on the advice of their county forester. Roads have been kept open for accessibility and fire protection. Ponds have been created in cooperation with the Soil Conservation Service. The owners have set out seedling plantations of red pine bought from the state nursery. They have thinned and weeded and sometimes pruned the natural forest. On several occasions, under the management of an experienced forester, the Rices have cut and sold under contract selectively marked timber on the stump. And the woods, in time, have profited from this care.

But bringing a woodlot into prime condition is a long and slow business. Proper woodlot management, according to Henry I. Baldwin, retired research forester for the State of New Hampshire, is like tending a summer garden. It takes periodic cultivation and a plan of attack to achieve the best results.

Contrary to a centuries-old European tradition, Americans have followed a policy of taking the best trees and leaving the worst. This approach has left most of New England—a natural forest area—covered by a poor quality of second- and third-growth timber.

Wood is one of our few renewable resources. As a fuel—and unlike coal, gas and oil—it reproduces itself. If only for its value as a fuel, then, the family woodlot can continually supply the homestead with enough cordage to withstand the cold New England winters. Even if not used as the primary heat source, fireplace and stove wood can be used greatly to reduce the need for other fuels. Hickory, white oak and beech will give out the most heat. Sugar maple, red oak and birch are also dependable. Red maple is less desirable while pine and aspen are both low energy producers. Green wood will burn but the heat it gives is low, and, because it may spark, the danger of chimney fires is increased.

A common measurement for firewood is the cord—a stack 8 feet long, 4 feet high, and 4 feet deep. Large logs should be split as soon as possible to hasten the drying process. Trees intended for the woodshed are often felled while the foliage is still green. Woodsmen then leave the trees where they are for several weeks; the leaves will help draw out the moisture content from the trunk. Later they return, limb the tree, and cut it into 4-foot lengths. Many leave the cords of cut lengths in the woods to air dry for several months (fuel wood should be dried four to twelve months or more before it is used), then skid them to the woodshed after the ground is frozen.

For this operation you will need a saw and an ax. Chain saws are common even among small woodlot owners, but a two-man saw and a bucksaw also come in handy. For splitting wood you should have a maul, a pair of metal wedges, and a sledge hammer. All tools should be sharp and in good working order.

January is the month to prune and trim, to weed and thin your woodlot, and to yard the wood to the roadside before accumulated snows of deep winter make access more difficult. It is also the time to skid sawlogs out of the woods and pile them conveniently so they can be trucked to the mill. But most small woodlot owners today do not have the time, the knowledge, or the equipment to harvest sawlogs. Cuttings are usually contracted to local lumbermen with the advice of the county forester. When trees to harvest have been marked and selective or clear cutting decided upon, an agreement for harvest and payment is struck.

Before improvement cutting

After improvement cutting

The demand for many woodlot products has diminished. Mr. Baldwin cites the falling market for wooden boxes, turnery, excelsior, veneer in small lots, tanbark and charcoal.

Sawlogs are still competed for, and in this fuel crisis so is cordwood for fireplaces and stoves. However, to the urban dweller, this is still a luxury item. According to Bob Breck, Hillsboro, N.H., County Forester, who has been covering the same territory for the last twenty-five years, stumpage rates (standing timber) have recently risen considerably. There is also apparently no end in sight for the consumption of wood pulp in the manufacture of paper products.

The small woodlot can supply top-quality sawlogs if properly managed over a long period of time. But it will take more years than most people have. A marketable white pine—20 inches in diameter at breast height—must grow for about eighty years. According to records Breck has been keeping, the average diameter growth of white pine—considered a desirable and fast-growing species—is less than two-tenths of an inch a year even in a managed woodlot.

"Most people don't even think about tomorrow," Bob Breck says. "A prime hardwood will take another twenty to forty years to grow, and when you start talking in terms of four generations to a lot of them, you might as well be talking about eternity."

He realizes an interest in managing forests for higher production has been replaced by a concern for preservation in the natural state—for trails, ponds, recreation and sports. "Because of taxes," he says, "mere preservation is a luxury few people can really afford." Breck believes in conservation, the keystone of which is use, but not abuse.

Pruning is often practiced to produce a white pine log that is clean and knot-free. (Another thirty years is added before harvest if enough new wood is to develop over the knot.) To prune—and often it is necessary if only to open up vistas, reduce the danger of fire or the invasion of insects, or to cut back trails and roads—use a pruning saw, never an ax. The saw can be attached to a pole up to 12 feet long and will make a neat cut close to the tree trunk. The ax may leave a jagged limb butt and scar the bark, thereby permitting easier entrance of disease organisms. Shrubs can be pruned with long-handled pruning shears. Experiments have been made using a club to prune both living and dead branches at various temperatures. But the results are inconclusive and seem to depend on the variety of tree.

Wood cut for poles and posts should be peeled to prevent insect damage beneath the bark while it is drying. This is most easily done when the wood is still in the green stage. Red pine poles should be harvested in May, not in the fall. This will prevent staining and rotting. In addition, in late spring they will dry out more quickly, be light to handle, and remain durable.

Thinning, weeding and liberation cutting in your woodlot are more necessary than pruning and have the advantage of allowing you to see the results and use the wood more quickly. These operations release prime trees to grow from 15 feet to 20 feet apart, increase the amount of sunlight, reduce the chance of insects and diseases, and release more moisture and soil nutrients. Thinning out unwanted trees—weed trees and those deformed, diseased and rotting—is not only good silviculture, but also will provide pulpwood and fuel, fence posts, and poles for the garden.

"Some woodlot owners," Breck says, "fight to save specific trees that are of no worth. They might be deformed and look like giant cabbages, or have heart rot or cankers. These should be felled to allow something better to grow in their place."

What should you, the woodlot owner, do first? Get in touch with your county forester and arrange to meet him on the lot. Go around with him and observe. Discuss the various possibilities your land suggests for developing wood products as well as some of the by-products humans and wildlife crave. Then cooperate in making a workable and realistic plan.

"Just keep pecking away," Breck concludes. "If a small woodlot owner would spend even a day a month in some kind of consistent weeding and thinning program, in twenty-five years he would have made a prime start."

But there is another value the woodlot owner can set upon his land—not because he owns it, for in the true sense of ownership he is merely its custodian for a brief period in the life of the forest. As Ben Rice says, "When I walk through these old groves, I find what I can find nowhere else in this troubled world—a sense of peace, of timelessness. The only clocks in the forest are the four seasons. Here, each moment is eternity."

References

The best reference for woodlot management is your county forester. He will not only give you advice on how to proceed but will supply you with information and material for study. You can also secure government pamphlets on forestry from your county agent and state university.

Reclaiming an Old Apple Tree

How to extend the life of an old apple tree—or even a small orchard—and bring it back into production is a concern of many new property owners. Although commercial orchardists think that any tree nearing forty is at the far end of its paying life, the one you have inherited may be more than twice that age and still not ready to give up. Often it only needs encouragement to produce.

There are two kinds of tree you might consider reclaiming: the one in your yard for home use and the one in the woods, either "volunteer" or planted before nature took over, whose fruit is consumed by wildlife. The procedure for rejuvenating is the same for both kinds; how far you pursue it will depend on your purpose.

So, before sawing down an unsightly but still sound tree, consider some of the things you can do to improve it without calling in experts.

PRUNING

Begin by pruning. The practice of cutting out unwanted growth not only makes the tree more manageable, but opens up its branches to sun and ventilation, regulates its shape, and increases its production. None of the other steps in reclaiming an old tree will be effective without proper pruning.

The only tools you need for this job are pruning shears, a fine-toothed tree saw, and a ladder.

ROBB SAGENDORPH

An overgrown "standard" apple tree that badly needs pruning.

Before you start cutting, survey the tree's shape from all angles. Dead, diseased or broken branches can be removed at any season of the year, but prune living branches in April and May before the leaves are fully developed so you can see what you are doing. Summer pruning (aside from removing annual unproductive watersprouts and suckers) is not recommended because it will reduce the current yield.

Most old trees are standards—tall growers to begin with—that, through neglect, have been allowed to become even taller. This eventually makes them impossible to tend effectively. In pruning these trees, therefore, you should first aim at reducing height and then at shaping lateral growth.

Lowering the tree can be done either by cutting out the center or reducing its leader and terminal growth only. Usually a combination of both methods is desirable. However, each tree presents individual problems.

After surveying the tree, decide how tall you want it to be, and cut a pole to that height: 15, 20, or 25 feet, for example. Stand this up next to the trunk to serve as a guide. With your pruning tools, cut off all growth that exceeds this marker.

Cut close to parent limb, angle for water runoff

All pruning should be done with sharp tools. Make cuts as close to the parent limb as possible and angled so as not to catch rain. Cuts larger than 1½ inches in diameter should be coated with a substance that will seal the wound: wax, house paint, or any non-penetrating, waterproof material.

Major pruning should be done just before or just after winter dormancy is broken. The tree's sudden spurt of life helps the wounds to heal more quickly.

Now you are ready to correct the overall shape. Decide how far you want the tree to spread laterally. Tackle the lowest limbs first and prune back lateral growth all around the tree at the same distance from the trunk on each limb. Then work upward, pruning each successive lateral layer a little closer to the trunk. You should aim for a finished shape that suggests a cone.

Even after the desired height and shape are established, you will want to remove interior growth in areas that are too thick. Thinning out old watersprouts and suckers will promote better fruiting. Do not nip off those little twigs that line the branches; the fruit develops on these tiny laterals.

Sometimes you will find that an untended tree, particularly one in the woods or at the edge of a pasture, has two or more central trunks. You should reduce this to the one best trunk by removing the others. If the tree was set out—not a native volunteer—one of the trunks will probably produce an old-fashioned name variety of apple; the others will be overly developed root suckers that may or may not bear the same variety. If you want to determine the variety, let the growing season continue and harvest apples from several different areas of the tree. Often the horticultural department at your state university will be able to identify the variety if your neighbors cannot.

New England farmers rarely set out fruit orchards in the blocks of trees we know today; cleared land was too precious. Fruit trees were planted in areas where the land prohibited cultivation: along the stone walls fencing the fields, lining the cow lane from the barn to the outer pastures, and near rock piles heaped up when the land was cleared. Browsing stock accomplished much of the lateral pruning.

Some of the most challenging trees to reclaim today are lost in thickets of brush that have grown up on land that was once open pasture. Many of them will have come up wild and will bear apples that are either sour or bittersweet. But they can be pruned and will provide feed for wild animals: deer, grouse, rabbits, squirrels, and birds.

FERTILIZING AND MULCHING

All plants benefit from the stimulus of plant food supplements occasionally. This can be provided apple trees by applying commercial fertilizer or barnyard manure in a band around the tree along the drip line where the feeder roots are concentrated. If the old tree is growing on the lawn or at the edge of the garden, it will not need more fertilizer than is given the surrounding area. Do not apply fertilizer the same year you have done major pruning. However, each subsequent spring you may want to spread three pounds of calcium nitrate around the tree.

Laying a deep (1 foot or more) bed of mulch will also help the tree if it can be applied conveniently. Mulch (old hay, bark, etc.) from the base of the trunk to the drip line will help conserve moisture and should be renewed as it rots to prevent weed growth. However, straw mulch often encourages rodents to nest and feed near the base of the tree in the winter. The trunk should be checked periodically for possible damage and, if noted, you should set traps and poison baits. For young trees it is essential to surround the base of the trunk up to the projected snow line with wire mesh to prevent mice from girdling the trunk and causing the tree to die.

SPRAYING

Each homeowner must decide for himself whether or not to embark on a regular spray program that will encourage higher quality apple production and keep the foliage healthy. A continuous debate rages today between environmentalists who tend to condemn any spraying out of hand, and commercial growers whose livelihood is dependent on producing the blemish-free, high-quality fruit that consumers demand.

A federal law with a four-year implementation date that has been extended one year was passed in 1972 and establishes standards for the use of pesticides in all fifty states. It divides sprays into two categories: restricted and general use. The former are stronger, more effective, and usually more dangerous to man and the environment. Permits to use restricted pesticides will be issued only to those who have taken a no-charge refresher course and an examination. These courses are conducted by state cooperative extension services on a county-by-county basis.

The question of whether or not to spray will affect the home producer of apples—who can still buy general-use pesticides from garden centers and farm suppliers—less than his commercial counterpart. There is little doubt that carrying on some kind of spray program to control insects and diseases will result in bigger and more salable fruit. Talk the spraying question over with your County Agent.

Still, the homesteader who wants a supply of fruit for his own use only might better direct his energies toward educating his family to eat good-tasting apples that might be misshapen, wormy, or covered with scab.

If you decide to spray, the only equipment you will need is a simple attachment to your garden hose, which gives good results.

GRAFTING

Grafting is still another—and perhaps the ultimate—way to give new life to your old tree. It may also introduce you to a fascinating avocation. This art was practiced widely by farmers before large-scale commercial nurseries made it a science. It is still the principal way of propagating apple trees and programming the size of the trees at maturity.

Grafting unites a part of one plant *(scion)* to another *(stock)* and keeps them in place until they grow together to form a single plant. It is best done at the beginning of or during the growing season when the bark "slips" or is loose enough to be worked. The scion is a bud or portion of stem that is fitted into the stock—the rooted or supporting part of the second plant—so that the cambium layers of both are in close contact. The cambium lies between the bark and the wood.

Many types of grafts have been developed to meet different situations. For the neophyte, however, *budding* and *whip grafting* are usually sufficient. *Bridge grafting* is also used when it is necessary to bypass damage to the trunk caused by rodents or garden implements. This technique can save an established tree.

To graft an old tree you will need a thin-bladed sharp knife, pruning shears, asphalt grafting compound, and a supply of rubber bands or adhesive tape.

A supply of scions can be either cut from living trees or purchased from a commercial nursery. These must be in the dormant state and stored carefully so as not to dry out until ready to use. Twigs about a foot long and the diameter of a pencil are best.

To WHIP GRAFT: Use scions that are equal to or smaller than the diameter of the stock. Make a sloping cut through the scion about 1½ inches long. Make a slit about ½ inch long into the surface of this cut. Cut each scion about 4 inches long so as to include three or four buds. Prepare the end of the stock in the same way. Join the two parts by slipping the tongue of the scion into the tongue of the stock. Wrap the graft firmly with rubber bands or tape, and apply a compound to make this junction airtight and watertight. This should be removed as soon as the scion has started to grow.

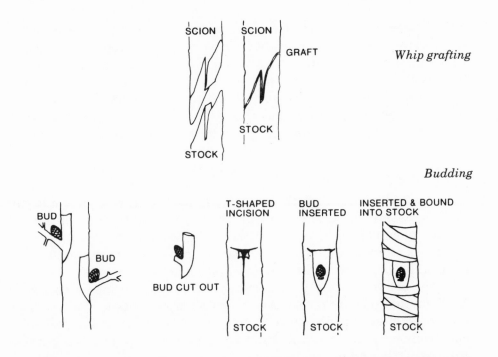

Whip grafting

Budding

To BUD GRAFT: Select a twig of this year's growth with well-developed buds just before you are ready to make your grafts. Cut as many buds from this as you are going to use by upending the twig and beginning your cut about ½ inch below the bud and ending about ½ inch above it. The cut should include a small amount of wood. Remove the bud from the twig, trim off the leaf, and leave about ½ inch of stem to use as a handle. Now choose the place on the stock that is to be grafted. Make a T-shaped cut in the bark of the stem and loosen its edges with the point of your knife. Insert the bud into the cut and push it downward so that the bark of the stock covers the bark of the scion. Wrap the graft firmly above and below the bud. No compound is usually necessary. In about two weeks when the graft has taken, cut the binding on the back of the limb and the following spring prune the stock just above the new bud.

To BRIDGE GRAFT: Ordinarily this is done only when the tree's life is threatened by a nearly complete girdling of the trunk. Trim

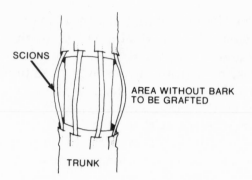

SCIONS

AREA WITHOUT BARK
TO BE GRAFTED

TRUNK

Bridge grafting

and remove all dead bark from the area of the wound. Use dormant scions longer than the distance to be bridged. Prepare the scions with double-beveled cuts at each end. Make an L-shaped cut in the bark of the trunk above the wound and an inverted-L directly below the wound. These will receive the ends of the scions. Several parallel scions are grafted around the trunk at 3- to 4-inch intervals. Hold the scion in its natural growing position. Insert the bottom first by raising the bark flap with the point of your knife. When firmly in place, drive a nail through the bark and scion into the wood of the trunk. Then insert the top of the scion in the same manner and anchor it with another nail. Leave a bow in the scions to compensate for trunk movement and to assure the continuing contact of cambium layers. Apply grafting compound or wax to each graft. As the name suggests, these scions bridge the wound so as eventually to unite with the trunk and continue life.

The art of grafting your own apple trees can become engrossing. You can add different varieties to your backyard tree. This will increase your eating pleasure as well as stagger your harvest. You can transform the tree you have inherited from a possible liability into a sightly and productive asset.

REFERENCES

Good sources of information are always your County Agent and the Cooperative Extension Service of your state. You should also consult the Horticultural Department of your state university. The USDA also has printed information available to the homesteader.

Cooperative Extension Service, "Budding and Grafting Fruit Trees," Extension Bulletin 508, Michigan State University.

Cooperative Extension Service, "Information Guide No. 8, Spray and Dust Schedule for Home Grown Fruit," University of New Hampshire.

Gardner, Victor R., *Basic Horticulture,* Macmillan Co., New York, 1951.

Hansen, Hartmann, "Propagation of Temperate Zone Fruit Plants," Circular 471, University of California, Division of Agricultural Sciences.

Langer, "Pruning and General Care of the Backyard Apple Tree," Information Guide No. 26, Cooperative Extension Service, University of New Hampshire.

Way, Dennis, Gilmer, "Propagating Fruit Trees in New York," Bulletin No. 817 N.Y.S Agricultural Experiment Station, Cornell University, Geneva, N.Y.

Designing and Building a Grape Arbor

Grapes are among the most widely grown small fruits in the world. Their vines must be supported to enable them to produce successfully, but an old-fashioned grape arbor will enhance your property by becoming part of your permanent landscape design.

The majority of commercial grapes for table and wine are trained on long, parallel post-and-wire trellises, but the home-designed arbor can be imaginatively tailored to fit any site—however small—and will serve as an outdoor bower of dappled shade or as a passageway between buildings to protect you from the summer rain. Your arbor can be built to roof a terrace adjoining the house or located at a distance, overlooking the garden. It can divide your grounds or screen unsightly places from view. Finally, the arbor will enable the homeowner to limit vine growth through annual pruning and to reach his harvest conveniently in the fall.

If you select a proper site and choose varieties of grapes adapted to your climate and locale, there is little reason your home vineyard—given some regular maintenance—should not last a lifetime or two. The average commercial planting in this country lasts from twenty-five to fifty years before it is thought to be uneconomical. The vineyard you plant for home use should still be going seventy-five years from now.

There are three general types of grape: the *North American* varieties (the most fruity tasting and winter hardy for northern climates, with skins that slip from the pulp easily and are not eaten);

the *European* or *Old World* (best known for wine-making with the highest quality fruit but the least hardy vines, their skins adhere to the pulp and can be eaten); the *hybrid grapes* (European varieties grafted to North American stock, they combine characteristics of both parent plants in varying degrees).

The varieties you choose to plant may not be as important as the attention given to selecting a site—proper water and air drainage are the principal considerations. Grapes thrive on sloping land with a southern or western exposure near large bodies of water. They require a long growing season and hot weather if they are going to ripen well before frost. However, they will produce under a variety of conditions provided the site is well drained. Ideally, they should be planted in a light loam that contains a substantial amount of organic matter and is underlaid with porous subsoil. The texture of the soil should not be so light as to encourage too rapid drying out. The fertility of the soil is not so crucial as its structure.

Air drainage is equally important. Although grapes are among the last of the small fruits to leaf out, the site you choose should be somewhat elevated so that cold air, which is heavier and tends to settle in low areas, will drain off in the spring and fall. Good air circulation during damp summer periods will also help discourage the spread of disease.

Commercial growers usually do not build trellises until the second year after an early spring planting, and then they use galvanized No. 9 or No. 10 gauge wire as support strung between 6-foot-tall posts spaced up to 24 feet apart. However, the home gardener should erect his arbor the first season, before the vines and their root systems have a chance to get in the way of construction. Traditionally, wood has been used for arbor building but metal will last longer.

Wooden posts—5 inches to 8 inches in diameter—were commonly cedar, oak, chestnut, or locust. Untreated, these will last from ten to fifteen years. If painted with a wood preservative or pressure treated, their useful life can be extended considerably. Another way to extend the life of the arbor and make it more stable is to sink the butt ends of the posts in 2 feet of concrete (5 parts sand and rubble, 1 part cement) that is twice the diameter of the post. Notch both sides of the base with an ax to allow the concrete to hold the post firmly. To provide headroom and allow for the sunken portion, posts should be between 8 feet and 10 feet long.

FOUR TYPES OF GRAPE ARBOR

THE LEAN-TO (see illustration): This kind of arbor can be attached to the southern or western side of a building and will provide shade for eating and relaxing. With one side occupied by building you will need to plant only the other three with vines, spaced not closer than 8 feet apart. There will be little chance the foliage will block early spring sunlight from the windows because grapevines are late in leafing out. The thick shade the vines will provide in the summer, however, will help keep the house cool. Use finished lumber or rough-cut posts and rafters from a local sawmill depending on your taste and your budget. Attach rafters to the building at right angles to the wall and nail 1″ x 3″ strapping in lines on top of the

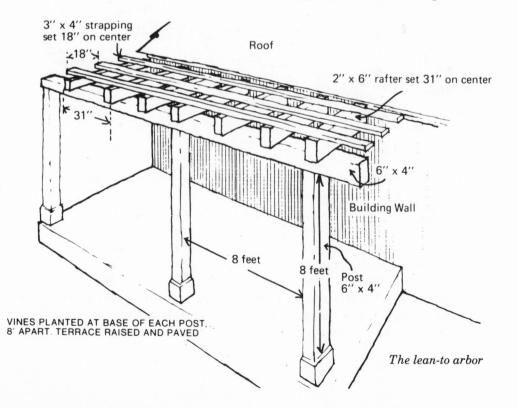

The lean-to arbor

rafters parallel to the eaves. (Remember to use galvanized nails throughout.) The finished arbor can be made less rustic by shaping the terminals of each rafter and applying molding to the base and capital of each post. Set vines along the outside, 8 feet apart. When they reach the rafters, space out lateral branches on both sides and tie them to the strapping until they establish themselves.

It should be mentioned that one disadvantage in having an arbor adjoining the house is that ripening grapes can litter the terrace and attract yellowjackets in the fall.

THE FREESTANDING ARBOR: Located anywhere on your property, this arbor can be designed to fit the site where drainage conditions are right. Effective arbors can be constructed above a retaining wall overlooking the garden and will serve both as a focal point and a leafy outdoor room. Determine the floor plan by its location and make allowances for principal walkways. Plant vines on all sides of the arbor but train them so access is convenient. The area under the arbor should be leveled. The floor can be covered with cut gravel or paved with brick set in sand, slate, flat fieldstones, or rounds of wood that have been treated with a preservative.

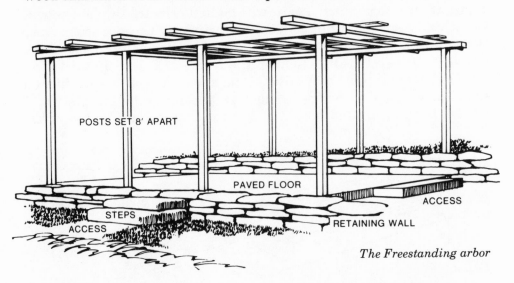

The Freestanding arbor

THE ARBOR PASSAGEWAY: Built as a walkway between two buildings such as the house and garage or shed, this tunnel arbor will provide cover during light rainstorms and help make the homestead appear more like a single unit. It is constructed by setting two rows of parallel posts 8 feet apart in the rows, and the rows far enough from each other to make a convenient walkway. The vines are trained across the top to form a roof. Given the space, all sorts of variations can be attempted: a central area can be widened to house benches and a table, or crosswalks planned along the length of the arbor to allow easy access to other sections of the grounds.

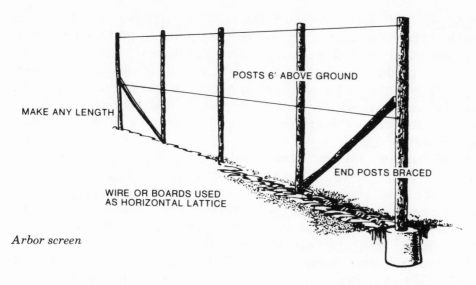

MAKE ANY LENGTH

POSTS 6' ABOVE GROUND

END POSTS BRACED

WIRE OR BOARDS USED
AS HORIZONTAL LATTICE

Arbor screen

THE ARBOR SCREEN (see illustration): The straight line trellis can be extended to any desired length. Grape foliage can be used as an effective screen in the summer, or the arbor can simply be used as an outdoor divider—separating lawn from cultivated gardens, for example. While not providing overhead protection, the trellis will cut down the force of the wind but still allow for air circulation. It can be constructed with wooden or metal posts set up to 24 feet apart. Three posts will be needed to support six vines. String galvanized wire between the posts in two parallel rows—the lower one 3 feet to 3½ feet and the upper one 5½ feet to 6 feet from the ground. A higher trellis would thwart efficient harvesting. If you prefer all-wood construction, set your posts at 8-foot intervals and nail on parallel 1″ × 3″ strips for horizontal support. The end posts should be braced to counter the weight of the vines and set deeper in the ground than interior posts. For an espaliered look and high production, train the vines in any one of the common commercial methods.

TRAINING AND PRUNING

Once the arbor has been built and the vines are growing, you will have to maintain them. Training regulates the growth of the vines; pruning regulates the crop, and usually both are done in a single operation. The commercial producer may use any of several methods of training (the Four-Arm Kniffin is common for most American varieties, the Hudson Valley for French hybrids, the Umbrella Kniffin for long-caned vines, the Keuka Renewal for large-clustered, upright growing varieties), which often are too technical for the home-use gardener who builds his arbor.

The first objective of the home gardener should be to establish strong-rooted plants and train the trunk vertically to reach the top of the arbor. Thereafter, annual pruning should aim to keep lateral growth evenly distributed and renewed each year so that the vines will be productive and can be systematically managed. Hardy American varieties can be pruned after the leaves drop in the fall but before the vines have frozen. However, maintenance can be delayed until spring even though the vines then may "bleed," exuding sap from the cuts.

For arbor vineyards, the trunks of the vines must be longer than for those grown on screen-type trellises. No pruning should be done the first season after the vines are set out. The following spring remove all shoots except those that are the strongest. Cut these back to two buds each. Tie the main trunk with heavy string in a nearly vertical position from just below the terminal buds to the top of the arbor, train lateral growth to fill in where you want it and keep this in place with narrow bands of torn cloth or string; do not tie too tightly. Practice clean culture around the vines.

VARIETIES TO PLANT

In choosing what grapes to plant, keep in mind your climate and your objectives. For those living in central and northern New England where winter temperatures fall to −25°F or lower, the American varieties will be the most dependable. Of these the Concord (developed 1843 in Massachusetts from a native seed) is still the grape most widely grown east of the Rocky Mountains. This is a late, blue-black, hardy grape. Others of the same color but with a slightly different growing season and size are the Fredonia, Van Buren, and Buffalo. The leading white variety for this climate is the Niagara, and if you want to complete the tricolor scheme plant the Delaware. A perusal of any nursery catalog will introduce you to the names and characteristics of other significant varieties that might be suitable to your situation and taste. Consult your County Agricultural Agent and the horticultural department of your state university as well.

Once your arbor is constructed and the vines thriving you will be rewarded with shade in the summer and a bumper crop in the fall. Grapes are ready to pick when their color is perfect, flavor and aroma are high, and the berries begin to soften. The stems will have changed from green to brown and the seeds will be dark. Even a small arbor should produce enough fruit to supply your table for desserts, for making fresh grape juice and jellies and, with some experimentation and practice, the material and incentive to make wine at home—one of the obvious benefits of the grape that has been praised for thousands of years.

REFERENCES

Many books and pamphlets have been written on the cultural techniques of growing grapes. Some will be more exhaustive than you need. The first step is to consult your County Agent who will know local grape-growing conditions and be able to recommend specific varieties for your area. After this write to the horticultural department of your state university.

Here are some publications you may find useful:

Annual catalog from fruit specialists such as Miller's (Canandaigua, N.Y.), Stark Bros. (Louisiana, Mo.), Kelly Bros. (Dansville, N.Y.).

Cooperative Extension Service Information Guides from your state university on cultural techniques and spray and dust schedules.

Latimer, L. P., "Growing Grapes in New Hampshire," Revision of Extension Circular No. 173, UNH, Durham, N.H.

McGrew, J. R. "Basic Guide to Pruning," American Wine Soc., 1973.

Shoemaker, James S., "Small-Fruit Culture," Blakiston Co., Philadelphia, Pa.

Root Cellars for Winter Vegetable Storage

*Harvesting onions.
Amherst, Massachusetts,
1915.*

The matter of storing garden produce using a minimum of our critical energy resources has taken on added interest in recent years. In northern climates it is possible to construct many types of temporary vegetable storage facilities: pits, trenches, pyramids of inter-layered straw and root crops piled at the edge of last year's garden, barrels buried in sand, and boxes stored in the garage or basement under hay and canvas.

For those who plan to stay on their property year in and year out, permanent storage areas are more convenient and desirable.

Permanent root cellars can either be detached outdoor storage buildings or an area right under the kitchen ell. If your house has been modernized with central heating and a cement floor, this may be a major factor in determining where to store your garden produce for the winter. The advent of central heating unfortunately spelled the end of effective cellar storage of root crops, which require high humidity and low temperatures.

For successful storage of vegetables, root cellar temperatures should be between 32° and 40° F, with a humidity of 60 percent to 75 percent.

Such conditions can be provided in a detached root cellar dug into a sloping bank away from the house, as was often done on early New England farms. Originally these storage cellars were made of stone, but today one can use poured concrete or masonry block walls. Earth was banked around the two sides and one end, and the

A detached root cellar built into a hill.

roof was covered with soil to a depth of 3 feet. A door, usually facing south, provided the only ventilation, and a bare earth floor controlled the humidity.

If the construction of a detached storage area is too much to undertake, anyone handy with a hammer and saw can construct a modern root cellar in the basement even if it has a cement floor. For the average family this should be about 10 × 15 feet. Use existing walls by partitioning off one corner of the cellar as far from the furnace as possible, insulate it well, and provide an outside window for ventilation.

Stud the two interior walls with 2 × 4s. These should be set 16 inches on center and sheathed inside and out with matched boards or composition board. Fill the spaces between the studs with loose insulation for use fiberglass batts. The ceiling should also be well insulated to keep cold air out of the house. Install a close-fitting hinged door.

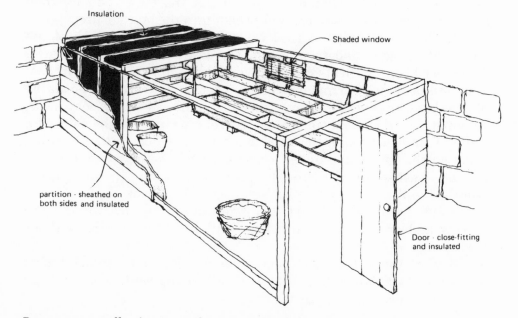

Basement root cellar (cut-away drawing to illustrate interior).

Pans of water and an occasional sprinkling from a watering can will help maintain the humidity. Light encourages sprouting; keep it out by covering the window with a shade or slatted boards.

If your house has central heating but the cellar floor is still dirt, the same kind of arrangement can be constructed. Should you have drainage problems during winter rains or spring thaws, it would be wise to lay drainage tile before constructing the root cellar. If this is not feasible, make a path of slatted boards to keep your feet dry in wet weather.

Some vegetables give off odors in storage—cabbages are the worst offenders. One way to deal with these is to bury them upside down in a trench along the cellar wall after they have been brought in from the garden. Another technique is to remove the stalk and outer leaves and wrap each head in newspaper, storing the wrapped heads in a box or carton. They will remain hard and firm until spring.

Here are some points to consider as you prepare to store your harvest:

1. Store only vegetables that are in nearly perfect condition. Handle crops as carefully as possible. Bruised or otherwise defective roots will encourage spoilage. While harvesting, set these aside for early use.

2. Postpone harvesting and sorting crops until the weather is settled and night temperatures are consistently low. Your storage area should already be cold before you load it with vegetables. Light frosts will not harm root crops; they often enhance the flavor. In early fall check the ventilation in the root cellar frequently.

3. After digging, air-dry root crops for several days. This hardens their skin. Loose soil can be shaken off vegetables like potatoes. If you wash vegetables like carrots and beets, be sure they are thoroughly dry before bringing them into the storage area.

4. Cut off the tops of root vegetables to within 1 inch of the crown. Rutabagas and turnips can be glazed with melted paraffin for longer keeping. Beets can be layered with *dry* fall leaves in baskets and buckets. Carrots can be bunched and stored in ventilated plastic bags or layered directly in moist sand, sawdust, peat moss, shavings, etc. Some old-timers core carrot crowns with the point of a knife. This deactivates the growing center, which is likely to become mushy in storage unless removed. After being cored, the carrots are washed, dried thoroughly, and packed lengthwise in wide-mouthed gallon glass jars with screw-on lids. Check the underside of the lids frequently at first. If condensation appears, unpack the carrots and dry them again. These will keep for months without shriveling.

5. Sort through bins of vegetables at regular intervals during the winter to pick out those that are not keeping well. Once spoilage occurs, it can spread rapidly if not detected.

You will see from the brief summary that follows of different methods of storing garden produce, that other storage areas will have to be used for some vegetables. Onions, garlic, and shallots can be kept in mesh bags or braided and hung in the attic or an unused, darkened room. Squash and pumpkin require less humidity and warmer temperatures and can be kept on the attic floor for months. Canning, pickling, preserving, and freezing can also be done each year to preserve the full range of your harvest. However, with a permanent root cellar, a variety of produce can be kept for winter use—if stored at consistent temperatures and humidity.

One final thought. Even if you don't have a greenhouse or a sunpit, once you have a root cellar you can raise a salad crop from December to early spring without either sunlight or bother. Grow Belgian endive in your root cellar. Raise the plants from seed as a row crop in next summer's garden. When fall comes, dig the long tapering roots. Let them dry out in a convenient place under cover for about a week. Then cut off the leaves about 1 inch from the crowns. Now plant the endive roots closely in a trench in your root cellar or in deep wooden boxes filled with garden soil. Water thoroughly once. Lay 6 inches of dry hay across the top of the planting. Cover with bags or old blankets to exclude all sunlight and wait. Soon the plants will send up new growth of pointed, close-leafed spears through the straw. When about 6 inches high, cut them selectively several times a week and serve either with an oil and vinegar dressing or braised as a hot vegetable. In return for a small outlay of time and energy, this salad green will add a little tang to winter meals and serve as a reminder that spring is a distinct possibility.

REFERENCES

Stoner, Carol, ed., *Stocking Up,* Rodale Press, Emmaus, Pa., 1973.
"Storing Vegetables and Fruits in Basements, Cellars, Outbuildings & Pits," Home and Garden Bulletin No. 119, U.S.D.A. (revised), 1970.
The Vegetable Growing Business (revised), Watts & Watts, Orange Judd Publishing Co., N.Y., 1951.

Some Methods of Storing Garden Produce for Year-Round Use

METHOD: Leave crops in ground and cover with thick (12-inch to 18-inch) layer of mulch (hay, dried leaves, straw) after ground freezes to prevent it from thawing. Crops may be harvested throughout the winter and into spring.

CROPS: Carrots, garlic, horseradish, Jerusalem artichokes, leeks, parsley, parsnips, radishes, salsify, turnips.

HINT: *Be sure to mark where each crop was growing so that when harvesting a particular crop, its location may be easily found beneath the mulch.*

METHOD: Build cone-shaped mound in well-drained area—spread layer of leaves, straw, hay, etc., on ground and place vegetables *or* fruit (do not mix) on top of the bedding in a cone-shaped formation. Cover with a layer of bedding, forming a vertical opening to the top of the mound to help control ventilation and humidity. Over the mouth and around the vertical shaft, pack firmly about 3 inches to 4 inches of soil; then place a board weighted by a heavy stone or brick over the opening on top of the mound. Dig a small ditch around the mound to drain away surface water.

CROPS: Potatoes, carrots, beets, turnips, cabbage, squash, pumpkins, celery, salsify, parsnips, winter peas, apples.

HINT: *It is best to build a few small mounds so that all the produce can be removed at one time for it is difficult to securely replace the earth covering after the ground has frozen.*

METHOD: For colder climates dig a pit (1½ feet to 2 feet deep, 4 feet wide at the bottom) in the area where the ground rises. Build the dirt around the perimeter of the pit with outer sides sloping away from the pit for drainage; then dig a drainage ditch around the pit to further facilitate drainage. (Remove stones from sides of the pit as they carry frost.) Pack dirt and dry, fine sand into the bottom of the pit 2 inches to 3 inches deep; on top of this place a layer of vegetables no more than 1 foot deep; cover with fine sand, filling crevices between the produce, and fill to nearly ground level. Cover the sand with a mounded bed of dry leaves, straw, hay, etc., held in place by a layer of soil or by plastic sheeting held down by 1 inch to 2 inches of soil. At one end of the mound, place a door on its side, slanting back. In winter, remove the door and dig in for the vegetables; then replace the door securely.

CROPS: Beets, carrots, turnips, potatoes.

HINT: *Never store root crops immediately after harvesting as they retain heat for several hours and may therefore not be as dry as possible. Allow them to remain on the ground overnight to cool before storing.*

The type of pit or mound you build will depend on the climate in which you live.

METHOD: Gather tender crops before first frost and store under cover in a cool basement, cellar or dry shed. Wrap individually in paper and pack in cartons, or lay on shelves in baskets or bins lined with a bedding of dry leaves, straw, hay, etc.

CROPS: Cucumbers, squash, peppers, tomatoes (you may wish to pull up the whole plant, hang upside down in cellar, and pick fruit as it reddens).

HINT: *Check crops frequently for ripeness and possible decay.*

METHOD: Harvest in fall and store in a dark, humid, well-ventilated root cellar where the temperature remains between 35° and 45°F. Place produce on shelves, in bins or baskets lined with bedding. A hard-packed dirt floor will help maintain humidity; otherwise, leave a bucket of water within the enclosure and dampen the floor frequently. Store the produce needing warmer temperatures on high shelves, and so on downward, with those needing the coolest temperatures near the floor.

CROPS: Beets, carrots, kohlrabi, rutabagas, turnips, potatoes, cabbage.

HINT: *Cabbage, turnips and rutabagas give off odors so they should be stored away from other produce.*

METHOD: Pull up on a dry day after the tops have fallen over and leave outside for a few days to harden, then bring indoors, store in airy bags, and hang in a dry, cool, well-ventilated area.

CROPS: Onions, garlic, shallots.

HINT: *Leave stems on and braid in long strands to festoon kitchen or loft.*

METHOD: Pick when mature but still hard, and store in barrels or boxes in a moderately humid area that can be cooled by frosty night air and maintained at about 30°F.

CROPS: Apples, pears.

HINT: *Handle fruit carefully and never store any that shows bruises or decay.*

METHOD: Harvest, leaving on a few inches of stem, before frost and bring indoors. Condition at room temperature (around 70° F) for ten to fourteen days to allow rind to harden and surface injuries to heal; store in rows on shelves in warm, dry basement, attic or root cellar, where the temperature can be maintained at 55° to 60° F.

CROPS: Hubbard, butternut, buttercup, acorn * squash, zucchini, pumpkin.

HINT: *Despite their large size, these crops should be handled carefully and should be stored without touching each other.*

---

* *do not condition*

Useful Animals

Keeping a Family Cow

When you are psychologically prepared to become the companion to a family cow—you will never *own* this curious rapacious beast—you will have taken a major step toward putting your home on a self-sustaining basis. For "tying yourself down" twice a day for at least three hundred five days of the year to a regular milking schedule in both sickness and in health, you will be rewarded with an ample supply of whole fresh milk and milk products such as cream, butter and various cheeses, a yearly source of veal or beef, and a mountain of manure with which to enrich your vegetable garden and pasture land. The cow is the backbone of successful homesteading.

Three common breeds of dairy cow for the one-cow family are the Jersey, Guernsey and Ayrshire. The Jersey is the smallest but produces the richest milk; the Ayrshire, the largest, produces the greatest quantity of milk, which has the lowest butterfat content. It is the Guernsey that is the ideal family cow.

A good Guernsey will provide more than 1000 gallons of whole milk and cream a year—enough to satisfy a family of two adults and three children, with ample skimmed milk left to feed a veal calf, a pig and a flock of chickens. An additional bonus for the spreading is more than fourteen tons of manure.

Ideal Jersey Cow

Ideal Guernsey Cow

Ideal Ayrshire Cow

HOUSING

Dairy cows must be kept warm, dry, and free from drafts in winter. Accommodations must be clean but not necessarily elaborate: an enclosed shelter with a window on the south side to provide sunlight, warmth and ventilation on short winter days; a pen or stanchion, and an area for hay and grain storage is all that is necessary to keep your cow contented. In anticipation of the yearly calving, you should also plan space for the calf to occupy until its sale or slaughter. The cow stall should be electrified; a single bulb is safer than a lantern. It would be handy to have piped-in water, but you can always provide for her liquid needs by lugging buckets.

Pens allow the cow more freedom than stanchions but will require about three times as much bedding (hay, sawdust, or wood shavings) and more of your energy to keep clean.

The barn should be wide enough (about 6 feet) to allow you to sit and the cow to stand comfortably during milking and for her to rest during off-duty winter hours. Be sure the doors are wide enough for the expectant cow to pass through easily.

FEED, PASTURE, AND WATER

Good milk production depends on good feed. Commercial dairy feed comes in one-hundred-pound bags with different percentages of protein marked on the label. Prices in central New England these past few years have ranged from $5.98 to $8.48 a bag. Your Guernsey will consume three to four pounds of grain morning and night. She will also convert garden waste into milk as part of the ecological chain.

Hay has been selling in New Hampshire for from $1.20 to $1.80 a bale (forty to fifty pounds) at the local grain and feed store. This comes to between $90 and $100 a ton. You would do better to arrange with a neighboring farmer to deliver baled hay right from the field for less than half this amount. This saves the farmer extra labor and storage. Buying hay will save you from having to purchase expensive equipment in order to raise it yourself, or the cost of custom cutting and baling.

A Guernsey will gobble up about fifteen pounds of good hay at a feeding while confined to the barn. This is about two tons a year. If she has good pasture of one or two acres or is staked out on the fringes of the homestead and rotated daily, feed bills will be less.

Fresh water must be available at all times as well as a medicated block of salt. In subzero weather the water should be warmed slightly to encourage the cow to drink.

CHOOSING A COW TO LIVE WITH

Once you have settled on a breed and have assured yourself that adequate housing, feed, and pasture (surrounded by three strands of barbed wire) are available, you are ready to scout around for a specific family cow. For the uninitiated, this may be the hardest decision to make. Locate a sensible dairyman in your neighborhood—one whose veracity you can trust—and pepper him with questions. As a producer, he will talk of pounds of milk; as a consumer, you will speak of quarts and gallons. Continuous high production, consistent milking and exact records are his primary concern. Yours will be steadiness, even disposition and particularly, good health.

By all means, find a registered animal that has been tested against brucellosis and tuberculosis, diseases transmittable to man. These are rarely seen in family cows today, but it is a sane precaution to take. Registered animals have been bred specifically for milk production and therefore are a good bet.

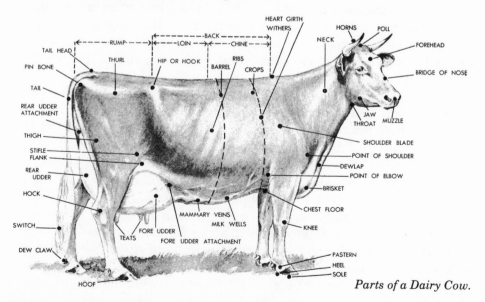

Parts of a Dairy Cow.

There are two ways of starting in: working up to milking by purchasing a heifer, or taking the plunge and buying a mature milker that has been bred, has already produced one or more calves, and has a good record. The former alternative has the advantage of requiring less money at the start and giving you time to warm up to the idea of being tied to a milking schedule (over the two-year period before she freshens).

Whichever way you decide, once a cow is housed on your property, your life will be changed. You must stick to your part of the bargain if she is to thrive and produce.

MILKING

To learn to milk by hand is a frustrating business but one that can be mastered with patience and persistence. The basic problem is that a cow has four quarters filled with milk, and you have but two hands. You can overcome this by purchasing a milking machine that will do this job for you, but then you are left with the endless job of cleaning up—which will take you much longer.

Perfection in milking comes only with experience. Essentially it is necessary to trap the milk in the teat by pulling down slightly with the thumb and index finger, blocking its escape back into the udder, working the milk down progressively with each curled finger, and forcing it out the end of the teat with pressure from the little finger against the palm of the hand.

Textbooks state that a cow lets her milk down for seven minutes as the result of a combination of circumstances that assure her all is well. These include feed, washing her udder with warm water (with a touch of bleach), and a gentle manner. If all signals are "go," she will start to produce a hormone called *oxytocin*. Loud noises, strangeness or hurry may replace this with *adrenaline* and the flow of milk will stop.

At the start it may take you forty minutes or more to empty the bag. Both you and the cow will be snappish and tired by this time. However, with practice on your part and patience on the part of the cow, the time will be cut considerably and, while you may never match the textbook record of seven minutes, you should be able to complete the job in about ten minutes. Milk morning and night. Work with and receive instruction from a farmer for several days before actually taking over your cow's milking schedule.

The udder should be emptied at each milking and the teats stripped with thumb and index finger to prevent them from clogging with dry milk. Generally it is best to milk at twelve-hour intervals, but your schedule and the changing seasons will determine this.

Although slight variations from time to time will be tolerated, the cow should be milked at the same times every day.

Even though you have a tested cow and wash her udder before and after each milking, it will be necessary to take extra precautions in dealing with your milk containers. Commercial dairy suppliers sell cleansing products. However, as a homesteader with one cow, you can do a safe job of keeping your utensils clean by first rinsing them in cold water, then washing and scrubbing them with soap, bleach, and a stiff vegetable brush. Finally, rinse and scald them in very hot water and allow them to drip-dry.

BREEDING AND CALVING

The most challenging part in the yearly cycle of keeping a cow is judging when she should be bred. The presence of other cows in a herd give the most reliable indication of a cow's heat cycles. Without them you will have to rely on a combination of observation, folklore ("her ears twinkle") and guesswork. Signs to look for are a sudden slackening in production (often by as much as half), a drastic change in personality (restlessness, bellowing, general rebelliousness), spots of blood at the vulva, flank licking, a glazed expression, and an unusual amount of tail switching. If any or all of these symptoms are present and it is about fifty days after she has calved, it will be her second solid heat period and time to call the inseminator.

Artificial insemination—one of the wonders of modern husbandry—is the only method of breeding that makes sense for today's homesteader. It allows you to choose the proper mate from among the best bulls in the country for either a replacement or a beef animal. Here it costs $8.00 to $15.00 per service, depending on the excellence of the bull chosen.

This means, if you are raising milk-fed veal and can do the slaughtering and butchering yourself, you will be producing prime meat at home for ten to fifteen cents a pound!

Nine months after your cow is bred she will produce a calf. Some four to eight weeks before this, she should be dried up (either by stopping milking altogether or by skipping milkings and taking less and less milk each time she is milked) so she can devote her feed and energy to producing a creditable offspring. For most dairy cows calving is routine, especially if she has produced one or more calves already. If any hitches—such as an extended labor period or abnormal presentation—should occur, call a vet. Otherwise relax and let the cow do what instinct demands. The calf will monopolize the first milk, or colostrum, for several days. This is not fit for humans but is loaded with natural antibiotics necessary for the calf and may be colored with blood.

WAYS OF COPING WITH THE MILK SUPPLY

You can pasteurize milk on the stove by improvising a large double boiler. Heat water in the outer container until the milk in the inner one reaches 145° F. Keep it at this temperature for thirty minutes. Cool it by substituting cold water in the outer container. When the milk has reached 70° F, refrigerate it.

Cream will rise by itself and can be extracted by skimming the top of the container after a day or more of refrigeration. Using a manual or electric cream separator will hasten the job and increase the amount, but cleaning and scalding its intricate parts may not be worth the time saved.

Once you have cream, you can use it to make butter. Churning is the process which brings together the fat particles. Home churns are of the barrel, dasher, swing or box types. An electric mixer or home blender can be used instead. Cream kept in the refrigerator for two days will churn faster than very fresh cream. Cool it (46° F to 50° F) and do not fill the churn or blender more than halfway. When the butter has come, draw off the buttermilk and substitute an equal amount of cold water. Wash the butter until it forms a mass, and the water is no longer milky. Salt to taste, put the butter in a wooden bowl, and work it with a wooden spoon or your hands until the salt is incorporated and all excess water removed. Mold in a butter press or pack in a jar with a cover.

A gallon of milk will yield about one pound of cottage cheese. The traditional way to start cottage cheese is to set fresh skimmed milk out to sour and curdle naturally. However, for more uniform (and less acid) results, start with one gallon of pasteurized skimmed milk and add one-quarter cup fresh cultured buttermilk. Set the milk container in a larger container of water and heat to 72° F. Do not stir. Leave undisturbed for fifteen to twenty-four hours until the curd forms and a watery substance (whey) appears on the top and round the rim. When the curd breaks smoothly when cut with a knife, you are ready for the next step. Hold a long-bladed knife vertically above the curd and slice through it from one side of the container to the other in ¼-inch strips. Then turn the container a quarter turn and slice again so the result is roughly ¼-inch squares. Now place the container in a larger pot of water on the stove and heat it slowly to 110° F in about thirty minutes. Keep the curds at this temperature and stir frequently until they are firm. Drain off the whey, pour the curds into a colander lined with cheesecloth and let drain into a large pot or other container. Finally, draw the corner of the cheesecloth into a kind of bag and immerse this in a bowl of cold water to rinse off the remaining whey and cool the cheese. Salt to taste (about one teaspoon per pound). Creamed cottage cheese may be made by adding about six tablespoons sweet or sour cream per pound of curds.

These are only a few of the ways you can use surplus milk in your kitchen. You can also make creamed cheese, ice cream and—with more experience—hard cheeses to fill your pantry shelves.

REFERENCES

Keeping livestock and using home-grown products will necessitate all kinds of reference books and pamphlets, many of them available from the U.S. Department of Agriculture or your County Agent. Here are some you may find useful if you're keeping a cow:

Cohan, Ray, *How to Make It on the Land,* Prentice Hall, New York, 1972.

Hobson, Phyllis, *Making Homemade Cheeses and Butter,* Garden Way Publishing, Charlotte, Vt.

Radke, Don, *Cheese Making at Home: The Complete Illustrated Guide,* Doubleday & Co., New York, 1974.

Rate, Hank, "The One-Cow Family Meets the One-Family Cow," *The Mother Earth News,* No. 15.

Stamm, F. W., *Veterinary Guide for Farmers,* Hawthorn Books, New York.

Keeping a Small Flock
of Chickens for Home Use

Despite the cost of commercial feeds, raising laying hens is an attractive project. A small flock requires little room, no expensive equipment, minimum physical exertion, yet can provide a steady supply of fresh eggs ("strictly fresh" as roadside signs eternally proclaim) and meat. Soufflés and omelets make great meatless meals, and even a twelve-egg angel cake made from scratch becomes a distinct possibility. Old hens and cockerels, culled from the flock, will put chicken on the table or in the freezer.

Costs can be cut by growing some of the feed yourself and by raising your own birds to replace those culled from the flock.

You will have to remember to collect eggs two or three times a day (especially in hot weather), feed and water your flock regularly, and spread fresh litter (sawdust, wood shavings, chopped corn stalks, etc.) to absorb moisture and check the start of disease. You also most be willing to study chicken habits and note any sign of abnormal behavior or sickness so as to assure your investment. Unless well fed and content, chickens can quickly turn cannibalistic. They begin by pecking at the weakest or youngest and soon are having an orgy of chasing and bullying with the first bloodletting.

The homesteader has more choice in housing his flock than the commercial poultryman, whose thousands of birds are isolated in individual wire cages and must produce or go. He may confine his small flock to a house all year or erect a yard to which the hens can retire on sunny days to scratch and take dust baths. Many prefer this to either complete freedom or utter isolation. Although hens left free to wander will have a more varied and interesting diet, they will cause havoc in the garden and problems on the lawn just where you may want to sit or amble barefoot.

The small family flock consists of from six to twenty hens. Permanent quarters can be in a partitioned-off section of the garage or barn. Or you can build a separate house. This should be constructed to make maintenance easy. It should face south for warmth and sunlight, be free from drafts and invasion by predators. Each bird should have 3 to 4 square feet of floor space. There should be one nest for every five hens, along with feeding hoppers, water, and roosts. A low-watt electric light bulb will help prolong the day during winter months and keep production figures constant.

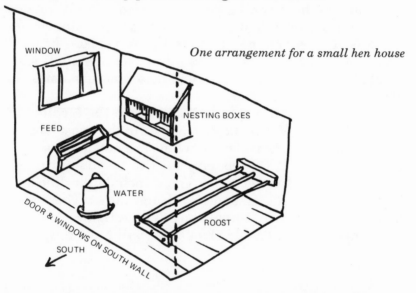

WINDOW

One arrangement for a small hen house

NESTING BOXES

FEED

WATER

DOOR & WINDOWS ON SOUTH WALL

SOUTH

ROOST

You can purchase chickens at various stages of development. Mature laying hens can be bought from commercial poultrymen when they are installing replacements. Or you can buy pullets that are about to start laying. These will be from twenty to twenty-six weeks old, depending on the breed. Day-old chicks can be mail-ordered from hatcheries and must be kept about six months before eggs can be expected. Many prefer to hatch replacements themselves. This can be done in a variety of home incubators on the market. Chickens take twenty-one days to hatch. If there are children in the farmstead, an incubator with glass panels will provide a worthwhile experience for them.

To keep a steady annual supply of future layers coming, you can let nature take its course. This costs nothing and only requires the cooperation of a broody hen (one whose mothering instincts compel her to retire to the nest for a sedentary life) and the sometime presence of a rooster. "Broodiness"—the instinct to sit on eggs until they hatch—has largely been eliminated from modern cross-bred hens. However, bantams, which are only seasonal egg producers, seem to enjoy spending long weeks on a nest. Therefore, bantam hens are often kept in farm flocks to sit on eggs, their own and others.

Whether or not a rooster is kept with the flock is largely a matter of personal choice and zoning regulations. Of course, for fertile eggs he is essential. But hens lay eggs without him, and often he has been eliminated through the mistaken notion that blood spots in egg yolks betray his presence.

Tending young chicks is not difficult, nor must it be elaborate. Buy starter feed from the grain store and make sure the chicks have plenty of water and warmth. The latter can be provided by confining them to a cardboard box under the wood stove or suspending a shielded 40-watt bulb above the box. Then, when they have feathered out, the heat can be decreased gradually by raising the bulb and after six weeks they can be switched to growing mash.

Mixed ages are incompatible in the chicken house. Therefore, until they can take care of themselves, young pullets should be segregated from older hens. This will mean more partitions in the hen house or separate quarters and yard.

If you prefer white eggs, choose one of the Mediterranean types of chicken—the White Leghorn is still the most popular. Asiatic breeds such as brahmas and Cochins are noted for meat production. Birds developed in this country tend to be dual purpose: producers of both meat and brown eggs. These include the Rhode Island Red, Barred or White Rocks, and New Hampshires. There are also many hybrid crosses, which it would pay to investigate.

When buying day-old chicks you will have to specify pullets or

White Leghorn Hen

New Hampshire Hen

Barred Plymouth Rock Hen

straight-run (a mixture). The latter are less expensive and the cockerels can be segregated and raised as broilers (eight to twelve weeks and not more than two-and-a-half pounds), fryers (fourteen to twenty weeks and from two-and-a-half to three-and-a-half pounds), or roasters (five to nine months and weighing more than three-and-a-half pounds). Capons are emasculated cockerels and are grown for six to ten months.

Once egg production starts, attention to daily care is one of the requisites for keeping it going. Water and feed should be available at all times. Unless you have a water heater in the chicken house, you will have to provide hot water from the tap during the winter. Fresh litter gives the hens something to do other than pecking at each other. They will scratch up the litter in idle hours in a constant attempt to rearrange it. Clean out the droppings frequently. Hen manure is a potent fertilizer and should be allowed to age before being spread on the garden.

The laying flock should be culled regularly to eliminate hens that are not producing or are laying at such a slow rate as to make them an economic liability. Learn the signs indicating the end of productivity: shrunken and scaly combs; strong yellow coloring of leg shanks and beaks; decreasing distance between pelvic bones. An aged hen contributes nothing but an appetite. She may live to be eight or nine years old but other than as a curiosity there will be no return for keeping her. Fowl—anything more than a year old—make excellent fricassees, pies, soups, and roasts if properly steamed before they are baked.

Unfortunately, chickens have the habit of molting, or dropping their feathers periodically. They are nonproductive while waiting to fluff out again. This may last from a few weeks to several months. A change in the feed, temperature, length of daylight, lack of water, or just orneriness seem to precipitate a molt. If you keep good laying hens through their molt, they will resume production. If erratic or frequent molting occurs, the hen should be marked for the pot and dispatched quickly.

Feed (mash or pellets) can be supplemented by strewing vitamin-rich garden wastes in the chicken house or run. Hens also relish soured milk, which adds calcium for the formation of harder eggshells, and table scraps. Of course, the homesteader with land and equipment should earmark patches of fodder corn, small grains, etc., for his chickens when he plants in the spring.

Because egg production will dwindle and stop during a molt, take steps to preserve eggs during times of strong supply. To test an egg for freshness, float it in a glass or pan of water. The freshest will sink first. Those that float are questionable—or worse. Eggs deteriorate rapidly and will absorb unpleasant odors, especially if they have been washed and scrubbed. This opens the pores in the shell and allows air to penetrate and decay to begin.

A cool cellar with high humidity (about 72 percent to 80 percent) is a good place to store eggs for several months. A glut in late spring and early summer can then be used in the early fall. Old-timers sometimes preserved their surplus by packing eggs in sawdust, small end down. Or they applied a protective coating of oil or grease and packed the eggs in bran and salt. One cookbook of the past century suggests using lime water for keeping eggs. This is done by mixing a pound of slaked (hydrated) lime in one gallon of boiling water. When cold, the mixture is poured over eggs in a jar or crock. Place a saucer on top to keep the eggs submerged. Store in a cool place. Renew the lime water every three weeks.

Another method popular today is to use water glass. No renewal is required. A quart can of this commercially prepared product can be bought in a country or hardware store. Mix 1 part water glass in 11 parts water. Use an earthenware or metal five-gallon container and place the eggs in solution—again, pointed end down—leaving 2 inches of liquid covering the eggs. This recipe will keep about sixteen dozen eggs. Store in a cool place and cover well to prevent the solution from evaporating. The eggs will be good for up to six months; after that the shells become brittle.

To use water-glass eggs, wipe shells clean but don't wash them. The solution will turn jellylike after a time but will still be a good preservative. Eggs may be added to or withdrawn from the water glass at any time. Some suggest that water-glass eggs cannot be boiled. However, if the shell has not become too brittle, prick the large end with a pin before boiling to prevent the shell from bursting.

A final method of treating eggs for storage is to dip each one in boiling water for five seconds and allow it to cool. Submersion at a more moderate temperature (130° F.) for fifteen minutes also will coat the shell with a thin layer of coagulated albumen and slow down the rate of deterioration. Treated this way and stored in a cool place with about 80 percent humidity, eggs should keep several months.

A final word about keeping a small flock of chickens is in order. Select a common breed and give your flock regular attention if you expect returns in eggs and meat. Start small. It is better to have a handful of hens in good production than a houseful of voracious appetites.

References

"Raising Livestock on Small Farms," Farmer Bulletin 2224, U.S. Department of Agriculture.

Rice and Botsford, *Practical Poultry Management,* John Wiley & Sons, Inc., N.Y.

"Seven Ways to Greater Egg Profit," Leaflet 327, U.S.D.A.

Kains, M. G. *Five Acres and Independence,* Dover Publications, New York, 1973.

Keeping Sheep
for Meat, Wool, and Pleasure

Sheep raising need not be a big business. Here in New England, a flock of from three to a dozen ewes and a ram, properly managed, can be self-sustaining and more economical to keep than most farm animals. Such flocks provide meat, wool, and pleasure. They combat second growth in the pasture and help maintain open space. Once the household needs have been met, surplusage can be bartered or sold to neighbors and craftsmen.

Traditionally, the farm flock is bred to produce a crop in the early spring, after the coldest weather is over and before summer heat comes to encourage parasites and discomfort. After being shorn, the sheep are turned out to pasture to fend for themselves all summer. Come fall, the ram is reintroduced to the ewes, and the cycle begins again.

Before the pasture greens, the homesteader will have experienced lambing. This is the high point of his career as a shepherd, when more and more time will need to be spent in the sheep barn checking the condition of the ewes day and night.

Sheep have the reputation of being difficult and dumb—especially when about to lamb, but others in the barnyard deserve these epithets more. Some ewes will appreciate a helping hand, particularly if it is a first or multiple birth, but these are the exceptions. As long as the shepherd is alert, his flock adequately housed and well fed during the five-month gestation period, and confidence and calm pervade the barn, there should be little trouble.

One of the first signs that lambing is near is the enlargement of the ewe's udder. When birth is imminent, the vulva will become swollen and red, and the ewe will seek solitude and be restless, circling and pawing the bedding. If the barn is crowded, now is the time to confine her to a lambing pen—a portable 4′ × 4′ hinged wooden fence, which provides privacy and restricts her movements. Once the ewe is in labor, she should produce her lamb quickly. If labor continues for an hour, the shepherd should investigate the cause of delay. Difficult positioning can occur in the ewe's womb, as it sometimes does in humans, and the shepherd will have to realign the lamb for normal delivery and/or actually help deliver it. Once it has been dropped, the lamb's nostrils are cleared, and it is encouraged to nurse until the mother takes over. Rarely will lambs be orphaned or unclaimed in the small flock.

It is also rare that a healthy animal is sterile. Ewes will come into heat with the coming of cold nights in the fall. Some breeds can be bred more than once a year. Separating the ram from the breeding flock in late summer and reintroducing him to allow him to run with the ewes for about four to six weeks in the fall, has the advantage of more closely regulating the lambing period (five months minus five days later). In commercial flocks, early lambing is essential so the crop can be ready for the Easter market. However, on the small homestead, lambing is often more convenient if timed for the first balmy days of spring, when both the newborn and the shepherd will be more comfortable during late-night vigils.

Housing for sheep can be inexpensive and primitive even in the north. All that is required is a shelter that is dry, well-drained, free from drafts, and has a southern exposure. Packed dirt floors are excellent.

The biggest expense comes in feeding. Two acres of pasture will provide enough summer forage for from three to eight sheep. When this goes, they must be fed hay. A daily ration of three to four pounds per sheep should be enough. Putting out more hay than they can consume will encourage the sheep to scatter and waste it. Many shepherds grain their sheep before breeding them, at a rate of one-half to three-quarter pound per sheep a day. This is essential for the ram as well. Others grain sheep throughout the winter or leave off and begin again about a month before the lambs are expected, working up to about one pound a day. A properly fed animal will produce healthy lambs.

Because of either lack of land or the cost of fencing, some flock owners confine their sheep to the shelter and a small exercise yard throughout the year, but daily feeding is costly, and this practice is as confining to the homesteader as it is to the sheep.

The threat of wandering dogs is the shepherd's biggest worry. Although he usually can be reimbursed by the town for any losses dogs may cause, this is small recompense for the decimation of his flock. Electric fences, hedgerows, and combinations of stone walls and barbed wire have all been tried to keep sheep in and dogs out, with limited success. Woven wire fence about 36 inches high, topped by a double strand of barbed wire, is recommended.

Consider your basic reason for deciding to keep sheep, and select the breed (pure-blooded or grade) that will most nearly meet your needs.

Although from the earliest times sheep were sacrificial animals offered to appease the gods—then promptly consumed by the worshipers—their ancestors were probably more like goats and were kept primarily for their wool. These small, rangy creatures underwent intensive cross-breeding to increase the quality of both wool and meat. This procedure was most successful in the British Isles, where it formed the basis of much of Britain's wealth in the sixteenth and seventeenth centuries. In Spain, at one point, exportation of the native merino, a sheep of unusually fine wool, was a capital offense. Merino crosses, especially from Australia and New Zealand, still provide some of the highest quality wool to be found.

For several centuries sheep have been considered dual-purpose animals, good for both meat and wool. Breeds have been developed that produce a good quality of both. The homesteader interested in keeping sheep is advised to spend some time reading, and talking to shepherds. Then he can make comparisons and select one or more breeds on his own.

If anyone in the farm family is interested in 4-H Club work, a small flock of registered sheep can be the basis of a good breeding stock to be shown at agricultural fairs. The sale of registered stock later on can help defray the costs of education.

This fine flock of Cheviot sheep, a hardy meat-and-wool breed from the Scottish Border, was raised in Maine.

STEPHEN T. WHITNEY

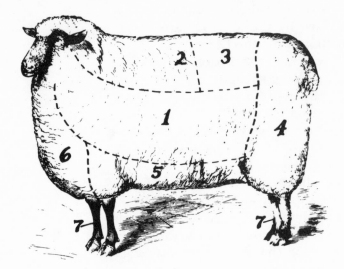

Meat chart: (1) loin; (2) leg; (3) ribs; (4) shoulder; (5) breast.

For the common homestead operation, grade flocks will produce ample supplies of both meat and wool. Registration papers do not appear on the table with the lamb chops, nor do they help you in knitting a home-grown sweater.

Meat on the table at little cost is one of the advantages country-men have. Spring lambs can be pastured all summer, cost-free, and slaughtered when they are from six to ten months old. Ram lambs go to the slaughterhouse first, for only one male is needed to breed the farm flock. Depending on the breed and age, spring lambs will return from thirty-five to sixty pounds of dressed meat for your freezer. You can butcher them at home. Expect to get two legs of lamb, shanks, shoulder roasts, rib and loin chops, as well as a good supply of stew meat. Or you can sacrifice some cuts for combinations that could include crown rib roasts, loin roasts, and a saddle of lamb.

Mutton has never been popular fare in this country. But elderly sheep (a ewe has a useful breeding life of up to ten years) can be slaughtered to provide a good supply of stronger-tasting meat.

Aside from the meat supply, the farm flock will produce wool each spring. There is an increasing interest in wool, as in all things natural today. You'll find that a wide variety of spun, knitted, and woven materials can be made at home.

Shearing a sheep would be easy if it were possible to immobilize the animal for a good long period of time (it isn't). You can shear with hand clippers or electric shearers. Or you can hire a professional (at about $2.00 a sheep) to save frustration and get the job done quickly. The wool should be clipped so as to come off like a blanket—all of a piece; this makes it easier to sort, wash, and process for use. The more second cuts (corrections of previous mistakes) that have to be made, the less useful the wool. The staple should remain intact.

Wool chart: the numbers 1 through 7 indicate the areas from which the best (1) through the worst (7) grades of wool are obtained.

Sheep are usually sheared once a year. (If left alone, they will eventually shed their coats in bits and pieces, which may be useful as garden mulch, or stolen by some birds to line their nests, but will not benefit the homesteader.) Some professional shepherds shear just before lambing time in order to check the progress of the ewes and help the lambs to find their mothers and nurse more easily. Shearing after lambing, provided the shepherd has done some hand clipping around the udder and tail, will keep the ewe warm if the weather turns cold again, and will be less disturbing to the ewe at a time when she needs peace and reassurance.

As a natural resource, wool has countless uses. Homespun wool can be made into an article of clothing, worn, washed, darned, and then—when other material would be discarded—cut into strips and used to make newer, larger, or more stylish articles.

If crafts such as spinning, weaving, and knitting figure in your reasons for keeping sheep—as they should—you will first have to learn to wash and card. Washing raw wool can be a tedious process. Some craftsmen prefer to spin the fleece after it has been trimmed and wash it in skein form. Wool with its natural lanolin is easier to handle at the wheel. Teasing and carding are steps to take before the wool is spun. This involves pulling apart the fibers and aligning them so a continuous thread can be spun.

Wool fibers each have tiny scales, which help them cling together and trap air and give them an insulating effect. Spinning is the process by which the fibers are twisted upon themselves in varying thicknesses, depending upon the nature of the fleece and the skill of the spinster. This can be done with a drop spindle, as it has been done for centuries, or on a wheel. The latter goes faster. Beware of buying an antique wheel unless it is in perfect condition or can be made so without great expense. They are likely to be either missing vital parts or so worn and warped as to be useless. Better to investigate modern spinning wheels. There are many on the market that you can assemble yourself.

Knitting home-grown sweaters, hats, mittens, and socks to keep the weather at bay may not occupy all your time or talent. The next step is to learn to weave. On the loom you can make mats, clothing, blankets, rugs, upholstery, and drapery material.

There are still woolen mills in New England that will take your wool clip and convert it to washed, carded, and spun wool in various plies. This process will reduce your raw wool by approximately one-half. If your flock produces more than you can possibly use, sell the excess at the regional wool pool, or save it for craftsmen whose location or zoning prohibit them from keeping their own sheep.

With proper management, sheep pay many dividends—even a small flock. If you love working with animals, and can develop the taste and skill for homecrafted products, sheep may well be a project worth investigating. And even if there were no other justification for keeping sheep, the frolics of spring lambs on a greening pasture make it all worthwhile.

REFERENCES

Teller, Walter M., *Starting Right with Sheep,* Garden Way, Charlotte, Vt., 1973.
Kluger, Marilyn, *The Joy of Spinning,* Simon and Schuster, N.Y. 1971.

Raising Geese
Guinea Hens, and Peacocks

Guinea hen

Pilgrim goose

Peacock

With increasing nocturnal invasions of rural areas by motorists, despite the energy crisis, some countrymen have arranged with the public service company to install streetlamps to flood their dooryards with light while they sleep.

If you don't favor streetlamps or a fierce watchdog but live far from neighbors, another way of alerting yourself to possible intrusion day or night is to keep geese, guinea hens or peacocks. These guardians will give the alarm at the slightest rustle of a wind-blown leaf or the approach of uninvited footsteps of man or beast. In addition, they will lend an exotic aura to your holdings and bring to your table luxuries usually reserved for festive occasions and to be had in this country only in sophisticated restaurants.

Each of these birds has been domesticated for thousands of years. Although guinea fowl are shorter lived, geese and peafowl have been known to carry on from twenty to thirty-five years. So, if you choose either of the latter as night watchmen, expect a long-term relationship.

A small flock of Pilgrim geese, a breed unique in that the sexes differ in color. Adult males are white with blue eyes; females are gray and white with hazel eyes.

GEESE

Geese have long been known in this country. The wild Canada geese honking in V-formation overhead foretold the coming of spring and the approach of winter long before colonists in New England were craning their necks skyward and speculating about the weather.

There are many varieties of domestic geese. Often fancied for meat and liver is the gray Toulouse. But Emden and African geese are also raised commercially here. The former was one of the first breeds imported; the latter has a distinctive knob at the top of its beak. Other kinds that are available include the brown and the white China geese, the Pilgrim and the Buff.

Whether geese are raised as guardians, meat-and-egg producers, or merely as farmyard pets, they demand little attention from their keeper. It is best to start a flock of geese by either purchasing a mature pair (from about $25 a pair) or buying half-a-dozen six-day-old goslings (about $1.50 apiece) and letting nature take its course. One course it will take is to tell you how many ganders and geese (males and females) you have bought, for it is difficult even among bird fanciers to be absolutely sure with goslings. Generally geese mate for life, but a single gander in a farm flock will be attentive to a harem.

Goslings grow rapidly. When you bring them home in late spring, they are merely fluffy balls with beaks and feet. Soon, however, they feather out, elongate, and come to fit their beaks. At first you will have to feed them *nonmedicated* * high-protein grain or mash, clabbered milk or bits of cheese, but as they and the season progress, 75 percent of what they consume will be in the form of green plants. Traditionally, flocks of geese have been set to weeding the strawberry patch. They can also keep down the weeds along the lanes and fence lines if they are started when the growth is low. They do not favor tall grass but prefer to work over areas already closely cropped.

When fall comes, feed them more grain (by then it can be daily pellets, sheep ration, or poultry feed); by Christmas a spring gosling will fill the holiday platter and weigh from eight to twelve pounds dressed. Most cooks agree that anything more than six months old is a gastronomic disappointment. Certainly, beyond the age of two years they should be kept only as night watchmen, breeders or pets.

Once the gosling has developed feathers and a personality, he can generally take care of himself. Goslings need only some crude form of shelter during the winter, for they delight in waddling around in snow and sleet and keeping the waterhole free from ice. A pond is not necessary to keep them happy, even though they are waterfowl by nature. Water for drinking and preening is essential, though, and some countrymen insist it should be available in larger quantities during mating season.

The advantage of keeping only geese as night watchmen is that their gentle criticism of noteworthy but not catastrophic changes during the night will only take the form of guarded conversation. But let fear become an element, and they will take their jobs seriously and set up a honking and a hissing that can be heard a long way off.

Geese have the reputation of being vicious. They have been known to attack strangers and to bite. However, other than in mating season, when possessiveness blinds reason, geese raised from goslings will behave with respect and a certain broadminded awareness toward people they know. Besides, they come to like their feeder. They demonstrate a wary trust whenever he appears and will often continue to follow him around long after they are grown.

The greatest disadvantage in keeping geese, even given enough pasture for them to fertilize, is that they often prefer fertilizing the ground near the house, perhaps because it is off-limits, or because they need some human recognition of the job they have been assigned.

GUINEA HENS

Guinea hens are another matter. These birds were first brought to Europe in the sixteenth century by Portuguese explorers from the

---

* *Medicated feeds or those with synthetic additives are poisonous to ducks and geese.*

west coast of Africa, hence their name. There they are still thought of primarily as meat birds, and although less abundant in this country, they are now achieving a sort of rural comeback.

A century ago it was a common sight to see a flock of guineas roosting in the trees at night about New England farm buildings. They are wilder than geese, more flighty in their personality, and much funnier.

Guinea hens live only four or five years, but their short lifespan is made up for by their loud noise, the delicate gamey flavor of their meat, and their looks.

The most common varieties are the lavender, pearl, and white. Of these, the pearl—purplish-gray feathers with evenly distributed white spots—is the most common. The necks and heads are bare of feathers, often highly colored with red and white, and somewhat scaly-looking.

They reproduce once and sometimes twice a year. A pair of guinea fowl will produce from twelve to twenty offspring in a single hatch. Usually the female seeks the anonymity of a shrub in the middle of a meadow or along a fence line. You will not see her from late June through July unless you stumble across her nest. Miraculously she will appear one day in the barnyard followed by a cluster of quick-moving little balls of down. They are so fast in their apparently legless flight to stay within reach of their mother's protective wings that you will not be sure of your count until they have feathered out and slowed their pace.

Guineas will come to a familiar feeding place for a scattering of grain in the open barn at chore time, but essentially they are insect-eaters and prefer to wander. During the summer they roost in shade trees, take dust baths among the vegetables, stalk before the glass windows to admire their prehistoric looks, pick at pea blossoms and ripe tomatoes, and mince away in a bunch when reprimanded or swoop off in a flurry of angry wings. When alerted to danger, they will fill the air with high, piercing, monotonous, and slightly insane chants in unison, long after what they feared has passed.

These exotic birds will roost in the barn along with the bantam chickens in winter. Or they can be kept in captivity year-round, but like all wild birds caged, are prone to flighty pacing that makes chickens nervous; the guinea fowl will always be the first to raise the dust when you enter.

PEACOCKS

Peafowl and peacocks have never achieved real popularity among common farmfolk in New England. There is something so other-worldly about a peacock strutting on the lawn with an open fan that perhaps the Yankee's heritage prohibits him from accepting a fowl whose principal asset is beauty. These birds are sacred in their native India. They have been known for centuries in China and Japan and farther south in Java and the Malay Peninsula. They found their way west with travelers in prebiblical times to Egypt. It was the Romans who first served them on the table. It seems an enormous affectation to serve a roasted peacock on a platter—his fan extends five feet tall and ten feet across—for such a meager portion of meat. It is said, by those who thought to live on beauty, that peacock meat is a disappointment—unpleasant, coarse and tough. For those who prefer exotic food rather than sustenance, perhaps a peacock served in full regalia is the ultimate answer.

For most who covet peacocks, it is enough to see them raise their fans and know their piercing voices will ward off marauders. You must live even farther out if you plan to keep both peacocks and your neighbors' tolerance. The cry for "help" a peacock raises when alarmed is so human it has led many rescuers on a fruitless search and driven off countless intruders as well.

Raising peacocks is a fussier business than raising geese or guinea hens, for the young must be taught to eat and drink if there is no peahen to show them how. One way to do this is to put colored marbles (the kind our children call "stickers" during spring recess at school) in the high-protein mash and water. The chicks will be attracted by the glint of these, peck at them, then somehow notice that food is attached to their beaks. They are also prone to blackhead, as turkeys are. This disease (carried by chickens) attacks their guts and will devastate both your flock and your investment. But if you get them off to a good start, your peacocks will be around for nearly thirty-five years, provided they escape predators and angry, sleepless neighbors.

Once grown, these semiwild birds, closely related to pheasants, are more capable fliers than one would think. They will zoom over the barn at any threat and come to roost in trees.

There are many breeds of peacocks. The one most commonly seen is the blue-and-green variety. All of them prefer parklike surroundings to match their regal looks. They must have enough open space to show their plumage as well as ample shrubs and trees to flee to. The sight of a peacock in full regalia on the lawn is breathtaking. The tail feathers support the plumes of the male—each dotted with an eye according to the wishes of an ancient goddess. These are shed in late August but grow back again by April. During mating season, and even at the suggestion of admiration from a passerby, the male will spread his train and rattle it eerily to gain applause.

As their longevity suggests, peafowl are hardy birds. They mature in two years and the females begin laying in April. They can also be confined year-round rather than be left to strut upon the lawn and take their chances. For this you will need a large, wired enclosure some fifteen feet square with a roost about three and one-half feet above the floor. This will allow the cocks to fan out without endangering their plumage. They should also be provided with a wire-enclosed sun porch. One male and two to five females do well together.

The cost of grain must be taken into account, for all semiwild birds need a higher protein diet than chickens get. And keep in mind the ever-present threat of dogs and wild predators.

There are still enough raccoons and foxes, fisher cats, lynx and owls to decimate our flocks. Skunks make their nocturnal presence known by robbing nests of carefully tended eggs, and dogs range the countryside looking for mischief. Of course, all these birds can be reared in confinement, but half the pleasure in having them is in seeing them run free.

A final disadvantage may show up later. You may find yourself addicted to collecting exotic fowl. In this case, your facilities will increase, your risks multiply, and your finances dwindle. Some pairs of birds sell for more than $400.

Guinea hens and peacocks are game birds essentially and therefore present more of a challenge to prepare than chickens and geese. Because of their wilder habits, their meat is likely to be dry if roasted like a chicken, especially if the bird is getting on in age. (Breast of guinea hen is by far the choicest part of the bird; don't expect much from the legs.) Therefore, lard the bird with thin slices of bacon, salt pork, or larding pork if roasting. Cook until tender, about twenty minutes per pound. Often more satisfying results can be had by braising the bird. This is done by browning it all over in a skillet with a little oil and butter. Lift the bird out and set it aside while briefly cooking a couple of chopped onions and carrots in the skillet. Now place the vegetables in the bottom of the casserole, enter the bird, and add salt and pepper. Before covering, lay a piece of buttered brown paper over the bird to help keep in the juices. Cook until tender or for about one hour. To make gravy add about one cup sour cream to the casserole juices. Heat while stirring, but do not allow to boil.

Very little has been published about the care and feeding of guinea hens and peacocks. Learn about them from a local game-bird fancier; attend county fairs and write down the names and addresses of displayers. Follow your local market bulletin and the want ads in newspapers. Talk with your County Agent.

REFERENCE

"Raising Geese," USDA Farmers' Bulletin 2251.

Working with a Draft Horse

Draft horsepower, symbol of a slower age and restricted horizons, once again has become well worth practical consideration for the small holder with limited capital and no mechanical inclination. Yankee hill farms are particularly adapted to the use of a workhorse. She can easily negotiate the rocks of small, irregular meadows and can maneuver well in boggy areas that tractor drivers would hesitate to approach.

How do you go about finding such a horse? One way is to visit a livestock dealer known for his honesty, like C. H. ("Cliff") Peasley of Hillsboro, New Hampshire, who has dealt with horses all his life, as did his father. He ranges from Maryland to the Canadian border, from the coast to western New York, looking for animals to buy and sell. After we laid our cards on the table—total ignorance, limited resources, a strong will to learn—Peasley shook his head and told us a good horse is hard to find.

"If you do locate one, it will sell for from $200 to $1000. But you won't get much of a horse for $200 today," Peasley said. Nevertheless, compared to basic tractor prices, this was a point in the horse's favor.

What age horse should a beginner look for?

"About eight to twelve years is a good starting point. After you get experience, you can go for something younger and spunkier. Start with a proven workhorse. There is enough to learn about handling a horse without having to break bad habits."

What breed of workhorse would be best?

"Go for a grade that can do a little of everything and not too much of anything. It doesn't have to be a swaybacked plug. But avoid any horse that has been trained for pulling contests. They'll take off with any equipment you hitch them to."

More important to the homesteader than cost, age, or breed is the horse's disposition. Horses can be dangerous. Finding a good-natured horse is important for the beginner, especially if he has children around.

"Working with a horse is a cooperative business. Your habits and hers will both take some getting used to. If you work her a little every day and let her see what you can do, as well as discover what the horse can do, you'll learn before you know it."

We refer to the horse as "she" as it is to your advantage to buy a mare, but even the ability to foal (in about eleven months) should not outweigh the horse's disposition. This, Peasley insists, is the prime consideration.

"For the home-production farm, there is very little a single, medium-sized workhorse can't do. It's better to hire out the heaviest work than to try to find enough for a team to do yourself. Provided you're not in a hurry, a single horse can do practically any job you set her to, including ploughing up sod land. You know, you can cover a lot of ground in a wagon. The same with a mowing machine. But you'll have to learn that you'll both need to rest."

How about the danger of working a horse too hard?

"It's possible," Peasley said. "A sweat is as good for a horse as it is for you. The only thing you don't want to do is work her to a lather. It's something you'll be able to judge when you get to know the horse."

Feed and housing and fencing are other matters to consider before you get a horse.

"Horses have to be well fed to get the best from them, just like everything else," Peasley says. "A medium-sized workhorse will take about one-quarter bale of hay morning and night and two to three pounds of grain while she's working. Some feed their horses at noon, too. Horse feed is pretty high now—same as everything else—but if you keep a cow, a horse will eat cow feed just as well." It's a good idea to supplement her diet with daily vitamins. Clean water should be available to the horse in stable or pasture at all times. A salt block should be put up on a stake in the pasture, or a salt brick installed in the stable.

How about shoes, vet bills and the rest of those hidden costs?

"With a lot of that you have to take your chances, just as you do with any other animal. You want to get a good, sound horse to begin with. She'll have to be wormed twice a year, and you must have the vet inoculate her for encephalitis, a disease humans can get. Unless she goes onto the pavement, there's no reason for shoeing her, but you should have a farrier trim her feet regularly—at least every two months. Of course, some horses go through shoes quicker than children. It all depends on the horse."

Only a simple shelter is required to keep your horse happy. Even in northern New England winters, horses prefer to be outdoors, as long as there is a lean-to or some sort of windbreak. (Some farmers keep their teams housed all year, they find grass makes them sweat too much.) During winter storms, cold fall rains, or daytimes in the summer fly season, horses want to get under cover. Housing doesn't have to be fancy. A lean-to is fine and flooring can be packed dirt or sawdust.

Grazing in summer is best done along with or after cows. If you are planning to raise your own hay, about an acre of the best land will be enough. As for fencing, two strands of barbed wire will be enough to keep a horse in her place.

Finding a good horse that you can work with is only the first step. Next you'll have to collect harness and equipment. Used harnesses can be bought at farm auctions or from retired farmers, but like all horse equipment, these are becoming hard to find. Harness should be checked thoroughly. Many necessary repairs can be done at home. Leather should be oiled frequently with neat's-foot oil to keep it in prime condition. Unused and untreated harness will dry out, crack, and become brittle.

The same scarcity exists for horsedrawn equipment. Many items have been converted to tractor use or left to rot when the last horse left the home place. You will probably need a plough, a set of harrows, and a cultivator—also a stoneboat, a mowing machine, and a wagon.

A wagon can be made in the farm shop with a set of car axles, two pairs of wheels, and some seasoned oak. Antique wagons—buggies, surreys, democrats, express wagons—in good condition are hard to find at reasonable prices. If located, they should be kept under cover, away from both rain and excessive heat.

Once enough harness and equipment have been assembled, find an experienced teamster to help you get started. The first challenge will be in sorting out the harness and learning the order and proper place for each piece. It also means learning not to undo every strap that buckles—only the key ones—so each harnessing up will be easy and orderly. And you may want to learn those names, like breeching, hames, traces, holdbacks, ridge pad, girth strap, checkrein.

You can enroll in a draft-horse school; a small number of these started up in recent years to keep the art of teamstering alive. (Write The Draft Horse Institute, Indian Summer Farm, Cabot, VT

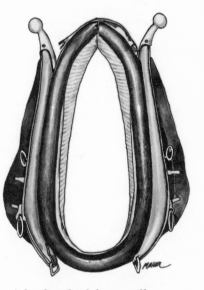

A leather draft horse collar with the wooden hames around it. The collar must fit the horse perfectly or serious shoulder galls will result.

05647 for information.) But the home-production farmer working with a single horse may find the best way to learn to handle a horse is to handle her. Persistence and regular habits are often the best teachers.

"Every horse is different," Cliff Peasley insists, "just like every man is different. With enough experience, both the horse and the man will learn to anticipate what the other needs."

Horses are large, intelligent, and very powerful. When working with a draft horse, take all precautions to guard against injury both to yourself and to your horse. Move slowly, speak conversationally in your natural voice, and make sure she knows where you are and what you are doing at all times. When moving behind a horse, place a hand on her rump or take hold of her tail. Never lift a horse's hoof without alerting her that you are going to by running your hand gently down her leg first. Horses like to be talked to—so don't be afraid to carry on a one-way conversation—in soothing tones, of course.

A horse also likes routine. Having done something twice, she will be on the way to forming a habit. Make sure it is a habit you want her to adopt. Feeding is one thing where routine is important. Feed at regular times. Never bother a horse while she is eating. She deserves the calm to enjoy her meal as much as you do.

Bribery in the form of sugar, carrots, or grain, fed from the hand, will sometimes get your horse to do something she'd rather not (be harnessed, accept the bit, stand still, etc.), but also forms the habit of expectation. Someday, if the reward is not forthcoming, you may be nipped, trampled or kicked as a sign of resentment. If gentleness and understanding can encourage a horse to respond, this would seem the better way. Sugar may become scarce; gentleness is a natural resource.

Some draft horses may never be well enough trained to plough a straight furrow or to cultivate without wrecking the planting with only the ploughman to guide them. If this is the case after repeated trials, use a ploughboy. Perch him astride the horse behind the saddle, and let him handle the reins. Or tell him to walk on the near side abreast of the horse's head, with the reins caught up short under the bit. If he can speak softly while walking the furrow and guiding the horse, all the better. The horse will like the immediate companionship at her ear while the working part of the job is taking place behind her.

Regional variations abound in the names of pieces of tack necessary to harness a horse for a job. There are equally various methods of procedure. Generally, though, these are the steps one takes, but they may change according to the type of harness and the temperament of the horse:

Throw on the saddle and breeching first. The saddle should be placed slightly forward of its proper place, then slid back. This will

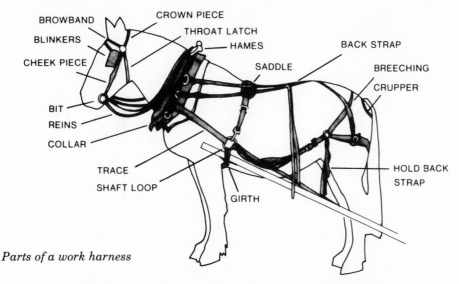

BROWBAND
BLINKERS
CHEEK PIECE
CROWN PIECE
THROAT LATCH
HAMES
BACK STRAP
SADDLE
BREECHING
CRUPPER
BIT
REINS
COLLAR
TRACE
SHAFT LOOP
GIRTH
HOLD BACK
STRAP

Parts of a work harness

make it go with the grain of the hair and hence be more comfortable. Thread the tail through the crupper and make sure it is not caught in the breeching. Buckle the girth. A horse will puff up her sides when she feels this restriction around her belly. To fool her, leave the girth buckle loose, complete the remainder of the harnessing, then come back to tighten the girth. Adjust the collar, throw the hames over it, adjusting them to the grooves of the collar, and buckle them from below. Hook the trace chains on the back strap to keep them from being stepped on until the horse is harnessed to the wagon, plough, stoneboat, or whatever. The reins and bit come last, once you have taken off the halter. Thread the reins through the rings in the hames and saddle. If the horse resists the bit by raising her head too high, with one hand gently hold the bridge of the horse's nose while you enter the bit with the other. In cold weather, warm the bit in your hands or in warm water for a few minutes before putting it in the horse's mouth; after unharnessing, wash the bit in water to clean it.

Horses' faces and ears are sensitive. Rub these areas as gently as you would stroke a cat. When grooming them, use a soft cloth. Proper and regular grooming of the whole horse promotes good health and circulation, provides the attention the horse desires, and gives her a sense of pride. It should be part of the daily routine, especially when a horse is being worked.

Horses are as susceptible to colds as people are; they should never be raced back to the barn. Allow them to cool off slowly and rub them dry with soft material. *Never* let a hot, sweaty horse drink more than a mouthful of water until she is cool.

Never cut the mane and tail before fly season. These are necessary to her comfort—her natural defense against insects.

A good-natured, well trained horse, *properly cared for,* is a joy to work with.

Food
for Our Forefathers

Fireplace Cookery

Cooking in the fireplace is not a difficult art to learn even if you have no experience and none of those venerable fireplace accessories like cranes, spits, spiders, skewers, jack clocks, and Dutch ovens so abundant in colonial kitchens and so expensive in today's antique shops. A few utensils are necessary but most of the necessary equipment can be found in your kitchen. The rest can easily be improvised while someone is getting the fire started.

You need: a grate or hinged metal grill like a hot-dog cooker for broiling; a roll of heavy-duty aluminum foil; an iron skillet with a close-fitting lid for stewing or baking; an earthenware casserole; a drip pan for catching the juices from roasts; a meat thermometer; some noncombustible butcher's twine, and a supply of dry firewood or charcoal.

Use birch or any hardwood for a good cooking fire, but wait until the fire has burned down to an overall glow with very little flame before starting to cook over it. (The same applies to charcoal.)

Fireplace cooking can be used for much more than just frying or grilling fish or meats (chops, steaks, hamburgers) or wrapping potatoes in aluminum foil packages to cook on top of a grill. Nearly anything prepared on the kitchen range or in its oven can be cooked before an open fire indoors, although a little more time (fifteen minutes to a half-hour more than oven cooking) will be required.

Thus, an unexpected power failure need not prevent you from serving the same menu you were planning before the lights went out. If, for instance, you were planning an oven-cooked meal—a casserole, stew or roast—for the main course, start your fire and make a "quick-and-easy" reflecting oven. Use a cookie sheet or find a board about 2 feet long and 1½ feet wide. Cover it with aluminum foil to reflect the heat and prevent the board from catching fire. With bricks or a short log, prop the reflector in front of the fire so you can adjust it to a nearly perpendicular angle. Then, with sheets of foil make vertical "wings" along each end of the board and seal a narrower piece across the top (see illustration for reflecting oven).

In the early nineteenth century, reflecting ovens were made of tin and included interior spits and hooks from which small game birds or skewer meats could be suspended—similar to the modern rotisserie.

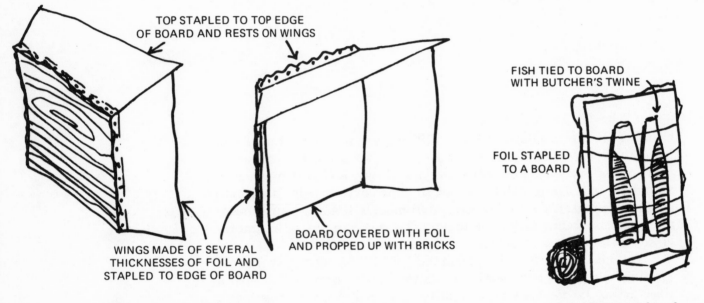

Homemade reflecting oven

Reflecting board

The Dutch oven is another kind of roasting device. This was either a built-in feature at one side of the fireplace (with or without a hinged metal door) or an iron pot with a close-fitting and slightly concave lid on which to heap live coals. If you have a heavy iron frying pan but no lid, you can construct an adequate Dutch oven by covering the pan with several thicknesses of foil sealed around the perimeter.

With only a few basic utensils and some forks, spoons or ladles, you can serve a wide variety of meals. Here are several sample dinners that can be altered to suit your taste.

SCALLOPED POTATO AND HAM CASSEROLE OR STEW
CANNED VEGETABLES
IRISH GRIDDLE SCONES
CUPCAKES AND COFFEE

MAIN DISH

Prepare your casserole as usual and place it covered on the hearth within a reflecting oven. Rotate it three or four times to assure even cooking. Time: about one-and-a-half hours.

To make a stew, brown or braise your meat in oil with onions in an iron skillet or heavy frying pan on a bed of hot coals. Add liquid, vegetables, and seasoning. Cover and place the skillet in the reflecting oven. The time will be about the same as if you had cooked it in the kitchen oven.

VEGETABLES

Canned corn, beans, peas, carrots, etc., can be drained, seasoned and sealed in individual aluminum foil packages and placed on the hot coals until hot. Or put vegetables into an earthenware casserole to warm on a bed of hot coals that have been raked out to one side of the hearth.

IRISH GRIDDLE SCONES

(4 cups flour, 1 teaspoon each sugar, baking soda, and salt. Add 2 cups milk and knead lightly for five minutes. Pat into rounds ½ inch thick.) Preheat the frying pan by setting it on hot coals. Place the scones in it and cook about seven minutes on each side. Butter and serve.

IRON SKILLET

CUPCAKES

While you are eating the main course, preheat your Dutch oven by burying it in the fire and heaping the lid with live coals. Pour the batter into a greased six-muffin tin. Place the tin in the Dutch oven, cover, and reheap the lid with coals. Cook twenty to twenty-five minutes. Sprinkle brown sugar on the cupcakes when cooked, and with firetongs pass a hot ember back and forth above them to melt or glaze the sugar.

DUTCH OVEN

The use of aluminum foil is a bow to modern convenience. In colonial times, of course, other packaging materials were used. Parchment was common. The Indians soaked green cornhusks and wrapped them around food to be cooked. In other cultures cabbage leaves that had been wilted in boiling water for a few minutes or grape or papaya leaves were used to make envelopes. However, today it is easier and quicker to use foil.

For a good cup of coffee, if the power failure has caught you without either instant or a drip pot, try this recipe:

1 cup coffee
1 cup cold water
1 egg
6 cups boiling water

Beat the egg slightly. Dilute it with ½ cup cold water, add crushed egg shell, and mix with coffee. Pour into a pot, add boiling water and stir. Place the pot on hot coals and boil three minutes. If only heated and not boiled, the coffee will be cloudy; if boiled too long, tannic acid will develop and make it bitter. If you are using a coffee pot rather than a saucepan, pour some coffee into a cup to make sure the spout is free from grounds. Return the coffee to the pot and repeat. Add the remaining cold water (to perfect clarification) and let the pot stand for ten minutes on the hearth where it will stay hot but not boil.

Planked fish is easy to prepare before an open fire. This need not be so hot a fire as you require for cooking meats, for fish should cook slowly and evenly. The taste will be entirely different from anything normally prepared on today's kitchen range.

Here is a sample menu with fish:

BROILING RACK

PLANKED FISH
(MACKEREL, SALMON, TROUT, ETC.)
VEGETABLES
(POTATOES, ONIONS, TOMATOES)
BISCUITS AND BAKED BANANAS

PLANKED FISH

Remove the head and tail from a whole fish, split lengthwise, butterfly, and tie in several places, skin side down, to a foil-covered reflecting board or cookie sheet. Brush with butter or oil, sprinkle with salt, pepper, and such herbs as fennel and lemon balm. Prop the plank at a steep angle before a fire that has burned down to glowing coals. Brush several times with melted butter or oil. When the flesh flakes easily, it is done. Time: about thirty-five minutes.

VEGETABLES

Wrap potatoes and peeled onions separately in double thicknesses of foil and seal. Place on top of coals and turn several times while cooking. Time: thirty-five minutes. Halve, salt and pepper whole tomatoes (add a pinch of fresh or dried basil) before sealing in double foil. Time: ten minutes.

BISCUITS

Make a biscuit batter and follow the procedure for cooking cupcakes.

BANANAS

Line up whole bananas in their peels on the hearth before the fire. Turn once. When the skins are black (about six minutes), split them open lengthwise, sprinkle with sugar and cinnamon (a dash of rum can be added at this point) and eat them from the skins with a spoon.

Pictures of a colonial fireplace seem always to include a succulent roast in the foreground. You can serve a praiseworthy roast from the hearth with no more equipment than a piece of butcher's twine, a drip pan, and a homemade reflecting oven. Horizontal spits were used in earlier times. Later, meat was suspended on vertical-type spits and operated by boys or trained dogs, clockwork jacks, or a heat vane that rotated the meat by means of the hot draught in the chimney. But today, hang the roast on a string attached to the damper handle. Its weight will cause the meat to roast on a string attached to the damper handle. Its weight will cause the meat to rotate with only occasional help from the cook. The drip pan will catch the juices and be handy for roasting potatoes.

Truss the meat (beef, lamb, ham, fowl, or wild game) with butcher's twine (meat shrinks in the cooking process) and suspend it before the fire within the reflecting oven.

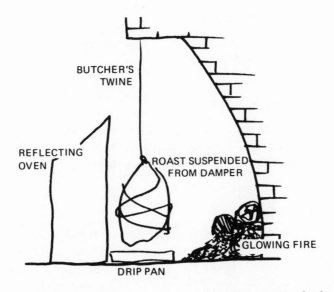

Roasting meat in the fireplace

LEG OF LAMB (5 lbs. with bone)
ASH-COOKED POTATOES
ACORN SQUASH
GRILLED PEPPERS
JOHNNY CAKE
APPLE UPSIDE-DOWN CAKE

LEG OF LAMB

Salt and pepper a bone-in leg of lamb at room temperature, Insert several slivers of garlic clove in the meat. With a trussing needle or skewer, thread a piece of butcher's twine through the small end of the roast, and insert a meat thermometer for accuracy. Hang it over a pan so it is suspended 6 inches to 8 inches from a hot fire and 2 inches above the hearth. Place the reflecting oven around it, wind the string occasionally. It will be ready to serve in about two hours.

POTATOES

DRIP PAN

Either cook peeled, cut-up potatoes in the drip pan for about 1½ hours, turning occasionally, or bury unpeeled potatoes in the ashes to one side. Heaped with coals, they will be done in seventy-five to ninety minutes.

ACORN OR WINTER SQUASH

(Or any vegetable with a thick skin) can also be cooked in the ashes for about sixty minutes.

GRILLED PEPPERS

Stick whole green peppers on a roasting fork or skewer and turn until completely charred. The skin can then be easily removed. Quarter and serve with butter, salt, pepper, and a little oil.

JOHNNY CAKE

This can be cooked on a foil-covered board or cookie sheet at one side of the fire. To prevent the cakes from sliding, the batter will have to be thicker than usual. Make the batter by combining 1 egg, ½ teaspoon salt, ¼ cup sugar, 1 teaspoon baking powder, 1 cup flour, 1 cup cornmeal, with enough milk to make a stiff dough. Stir together. Form into cakes ½ inch thick and place them on the board near the fire so they can dry out and set slightly. When they have set, prop the board at an angle before hot coals.

Adjust it as the cakes nearest the heat begin to brown. It is not necessary to turn the cakes themselves. In about twenty minutes, split, spread with butter or honey, and serve.

APPLES

Can be baked. Core, fill with brown sugar, raisins and a pat of butter. Then wrap and seal in double thicknesses of foil. Lay them in hot coals under the burning logs for about thirty minutes.

Another fireplace apple dessert is an upside-down cake. As you preheat the lid of an iron frying pan, spread 4 tablespoons butter on the bottom of the pan. Pare and slice enough apples to cover the bottom, sprinkle them with ½ cup sugar and 1 teaspoon cinnamon. Pour on a batter made with 1 cup flour sifted with 1½ teaspoons baking powder, ½ teaspoon salt, ¼ cup butter and ½ cup sugar. Add 1 egg and then the dry ingredients to ½ cup milk and 1 teaspoon vanilla. Now rake out enough hot coals to one side of the fire to make a bed about 2 inches thick. Level the pan on them and cover. Heap the top with coals and bank the sides of the pan. Time: about one hour.

There are many other vegetables that can be cooked before an open fire without being boiled. Variety depending on the season will provide balanced and interesting meals. And any meal is complemented by a fresh salad. Without the pressure of an emergency such as a power failure, a little prior experience in timing is all that will be needed to turn out from the fireplace a gourmet meal of several courses featuring different sauces and beverages.

Whole Wheat Bread from Grain to Loaf

WHEAT

RYE

BARLEY

OATS

Watch your knuckles and your back as the swiple arcs the air. Flailing is only one of the acquired arts you will have to master when making whole wheat bread for the homestead from seed to loaf. But—like chopping wood—it serves a double purpose. Flailing separates grain from straw while preheating the appetite in anticipation of one of the most welcome aromas to pervade the kitchen. The odor of fresh baked bread alone is worth the effort of preparation; a thick slice of whole grain bread hot from the oven, capped by a melting slab of butter, certainly stands as one of the most delicious foods of all time.

In times past, general farms throughout Colonial America raised small grains—wheat, rye, barley and oats—most of which were used to feed stock. Flour for home use was ground locally, but as labor became scarcer and mills closed, the practice died. Few millers ply their dusty, noisy trade along the waterways of New England today. Yet some still stone-grind grain and supply gourmet shops, natural food stores, and discriminating cooks.

Many kinds of wheat are grown for flour. Although sources suggest planting the variety that is successfully grown in your area, with grain-growing for home use only now experiencing a rejuvenation in much of New England, the best procedure is to experiment. Even county agents hereabouts admittedly lack the experience to offer sound advice.

Winter wheat is so named because it is sown in early fall several weeks before the first killing frost. It germinates and grows but remains dormant under winter snows. In spring it greens again and develops until harvest time in early summer. Spring wheat is sown as early in the spring as the ground is workable and harvested before the advent of hot weather.

Hard red winter and hard red spring wheats are used primarily for making bread. Soft red winter wheat is used for cake dough and pastries. Generally, flour made from the hard wheats will rise better and take heavier handling.

Despite the preference for spring wheat by bread makers, here in New England it would be better to plant soft red winter wheat as a first experiment in growing your own grain. In case the crop fails to develop properly because of local soil and climatic conditions, you will at least have gained a cover crop to check erosion and can plough it under as a green manure to enrich the soil come spring.

This variety has been grown successfully by Samuel Kayman, an organic farmer in the upper Connecticut Valley. He seeded an acre of prepared land and harvested four hundred fifty pounds of wheat, which he claims is a disappointing yield. After the seed was broadcast, it was raked or disked into the soil. Wheat will tolerate a wide pH range (a scale to determine the acidity or alkalinity of the soil), but must be planted in fairly fertile soil and be well drained.

Two bushels (about one hundred twenty pounds) will plant an acre. Before you begin your experiment, however, consider the labor and time necessary to harvest your crop—particularly if there is no local custom combine or miller to convert your harvest into flour. According to Kayman, one-eighth of an acre—or an area about 50′ × 100′—will provide enough wheat for an average homesteading family. For this about fifteen pounds of seed will be necessary.

Small grain seed is available through farm supply houses or natural food stores but rarely is listed in commercial seed company catalogs. (See list at end of chapter.)

There are two principal methods of harvesting small grains. Large operations in the wheat-growing country of the midwest use a combined harvester-thresher. But these are hard to locate to service small plantings in oddly sized Yankee fields. Probably you will have to revert to old-fashioned methods by cradling your harvest.

Harvesting Grain

CRADLE

A cradle is a scythe furnished with a set of long, parallel fingers for catching the grain as it is mowed and laying it in swaths. If a cradle is not available, an ordinary grass scythe can be used but the wheat will have to be hand-gathered to bundle and stack.

For home use, wheat is cradled before it is fully ripe, bound into bundles, stacked in sheaves, and allowed to stand in the field three or four days to completely ripen. Then it can be carried to a dry shed and left to "sweat" a few weeks or until you are ready to flail it.

A flail is an ancient farm instrument—once even converted into a weapon of war—that consists of two wooden parts: a long handle and a shorter, stouter stick called a *swiple* or *swingle*. These are usually hinged with leather thongs to allow the swiple to swing freely. As it arcs back, hopefully the knuckles of the flailer will be out of the way as he grasps the longer handle.

Flailing is usually done on a clean sheet on the barn floor or outdoors on a dry day. The wheat is beaten to separate the stalk or straw from the berry (seed).

After the seed is collected, it is winnowed on a breezy day by pouring it repeatedly from one container to another until the chaff is blown away and the heavier seed falls into a receiving bucket.

When this operation is complete (and the straw set aside for bedding down the stock), store your harvest in a dry, mouse-proof place until ready to be ground. Grind in small amounts as the need arises. Much of the nutritional value is lost if the berry is ground prematurely or if it is exposed to high temperatures.

There are several kinds of home grain grinders available. Hand-operated grinders—Corona and Quaker City among them—average in price from twenty to thirty dollars. Electric mills, of course, are more expensive. These cost from $95 to $245 for a large-capacity mill capable of grinding one hundred pounds of flour in an hour.

For the amounts needed in most home kitchens, either a hand grinder or a common electric blender will be sufficient. The latter will grind wheat berries into a coarse but usable flour quickly. Generally one pound of berry will yield a little more than 3 cups of flour.

The beauty of the hand grinder—with either metal or carborundum "stones"—is that it can be adjusted so as to regulate the fineness of the flour through successive grindings. A wing nut keeps the stones at set distances. Unlike the water-powered mill stones of old, these will not have to be redressed to keep grinding effectively. Many prefer coarse ground wheat for bread; it provides a nuttier flavor, a crunchier texture. Others want a smoother, finer flour. Your choice really depends on the recipe and personal preference.

Here are three recipes for whole wheat bread, all tasty and nutritious and well worth the effort of growing your own grain.

Baking bread is an art. Whether you make a loaf at a time or enough to supply your family's needs for a week at one baking, the

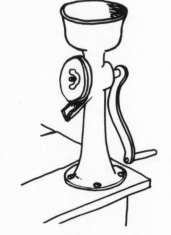

A home gristmill

results will depend on a set of variables such as the quality of the ingredients, the temperature and the humidity. If your first attempts are not too successful, or if your results seem to take a slump after several good batches, try again. Make all conditions as close to perfect as possible. Only experience will bring perfection.

The first introduction to bread-making may be in watching instinctive cooks practice their magic. One remembered recipe—taken at the elbow of the wife of a Newfoundland fisherman—uses terms such as "butter the size of an egg" and "a well worn sweat shirt" to cover the rising dough. The problem she did not experience was how to remove sticky dough from hairy arms. (Add more flour while kneading the dough.)

Another instinctive cook is Mrs. Scat, a frequent visitor. She adds ingredients by "feel." The following recipe is adapted from watching her. It has been translated into more literal terms to produce an excellent loaf with very little work.

MRS. SCAT'S NO-KNEAD WHOLE WHEAT BREAD
(one loaf)

4 cups freshly ground whole wheat flour
2 packages dry yeast (2 tablespoons)
2 tablespoons molasses
1¾ cups warm water
¼ cup cooking oil
1 tablespoon salt

Put 4 cups freshly ground whole wheat flour into a mixing bowl and place it in the oven to warm. The heat should be as low as possible. In a gas oven, the pilot light will do. Proof the yeast (to assure its viability) by dissolving the yeast in ½ cup warm water. If after a few minutes it does not bubble, throw it away and start with a new batch. Add 2 tablespoons molasses to active yeast and stir. Meanwhile, grease a 9″ × 5″ × 3″ bread pan with oil, butter or lard. Add flour, ¼ cup oil, 1¼ cups water, and 1 tablespoon salt to the yeast and molasses. The resulting dough should be sticky. If too liquid, add more flour. When it is thoroughly mixed, spoon the dough into the pan, distributing it evenly, especially in the corners. Put the pan in a warm place to rise and increase in size by about one-third. Bake in a 450° F oven about forty minutes.

(One hint for slicing hot bread successfully is suggested by Louise Dickinson Rich in *We Took to the Woods.* Preheat your bread knife on the top of the stove before slicing.)

Another dependable recipe comes from *Beard on Bread,*© 1973 by James A. Beard, reprinted by permission of Alfred A. Knopf, Inc., New York. This recipe originated at the Norwegian Government School for Domestic Science Teachers.

WHOLE-MEAL BREAD WITH POTATOES
(two round loaves)

2 packages dry yeast (or 2 tablespoons)
½ cup warm water
1 pound peeled and grated potatoes
3 cups buttermilk
1 tablespoon salt
6 cups whole-meal whole-wheat flour (about 2 pounds berry)
4 cups all-purpose flour

Proof the yeast in warm water. Heat the potatoes with a small amount of buttermilk, then add to the yeast. Add the salt and the rest of the heated buttermilk. Stir in all the flour, a cup at a time, until the dough is firm. Knead until elastic. Place in a buttered bowl and cover. Let rise until doubled in bulk. Now punch down the dough and knead again. Shape into two round loaves and place on a buttered baking sheet. Again let them rise until doubled in bulk. Bake in a preheated oven at 375° F until done (thirty to thirty-five minutes).

Finally, for those who want a sweeter whole-grain bread, try this:

WHOLE WHEAT BREAD WITH HONEY
(three small or two large loaves)

3 tablespoons butter
3 tablespoons honey
1 pint milk (2 cups)
1 tablespoon salt
2 packages dry yeast
6 cups whole wheat flour

Proof the yeast in ½ cup of the warmed milk. Melt butter and honey in the remainder of the milk in a saucepan over low heat. When lukewarm add the yeast and salt. Stir while adding flour until the dough is stiff enough to knead. Knead on a floured board for about eight minutes. Put in greased bowl and let rise until doubled in bulk. Turn out on a floured board and knead again for a few seconds. Then divide into three small or two large loaf pans and let rise again. Bake in a preheated 375° F oven about fifty minutes.

SUPPLIERS

SEED SOURCES:

Johnny Appleseed, Acton, Mass. 01720
Stamford Seed Co., 560 Fulton Street, Box 366, Buffalo, N.Y. 14240.
Rhorher Brothers, Smoketown, Pa.

FLOUR MILL SOURCES:

Corona Mill—Grinds corn, wheat, nuts, seeds, etc. Easily adjustable. Speedy and easy to operate. Heavy duty cast iron. Weighs about ten lbs., $16.50 postpaid. Electric flour mills for $179.50. Write for more information: R & R Mill Company, 45 West First North, Smithfield, Utah 84335.

Quaker City Mill—Flour on one grinding, $11.95 plus postage from: Nelson & Sons, Inc. P.O. Box 1296, Salt Lake City, Utah 84110.

Lee Electric Flour Mill catalog from Lee Engineering Co., 2023 W. Wisconsin Ave., Milwaukee, Wisc. 53403.

REFERENCES

Logsdon, Gene, "Grow Wheat in Your Garden" *Organic Gardening,* Jan. 1972.

Beard, James, *Beard on Bread,* Knopf, New York, 1973.

Raising and Drying Beans and Corn

Although any variety of bean and corn that matures in the garden can be dried for winter use, for best results plant those that have been especially developed for drying.

Raising and drying shell beans is one of the easiest garden projects. In addition to tasting good, beans are rich in amino acids, which make up proteins and are essential to our diets. A good corn crop is more of a challenge—and will take more room in your garden—but your own home-grown, home-ground cornmeal is a superb basis for fine dishes like johnnycake, polenta, and Indian pudding.

Both beans and corn are warm-weather, warm-soil crops generally planted when all danger of frost has passed. Both will need shallow cultivation at first to cut down competition from weeds. This can be done with a lightweight hoe, walking cultivator, or Rototiller cultivator. Later on, you can just leave them to "vegetate" until ready for harvest.

BEANS

Bush beans are planted every 3 inches in rows that are spaced 2½ feet apart. Pole beans are hilled around a supporting stake or pole and thinned to three or four vigorous plants after they have germinated. Snap beans, pole or bush, that develop beyond the pencil thickness that is the gourmet's delight (both for eating fresh and freezing), and seem to keep growing while your back is turned, should generate neither panic nor guilt in the gardener. Leave them on the vine to mature completely, and you will have a whole parcel of winter meals with scarcely any effort. Or save them for next year's seed crop.

If you are going to devote a larger part of your garden to raising beans for drying next season—a thrifty alternative in view of present supermarket prices for dried beans, until recently considered a poor man's fare—pore over seed catalogs and order beans specifically recommended for drying. These may include kidney beans, soldiers, Vermont cranberries, navy beans, limas, white pea beans, and soybeans. First, take into account the length of your growing season. Soybeans and limas have the highest protein value, but they both need a longer time to mature than is generally available in central New England. Occasionally, however, a happy combination of temperature, water, and frost-free days may produce a respectable crop.

Shell beans (another name for dried beans) are harvested when the pods have matured and begun to dry, but before they open and scatter their seeds. The gardener must achieve a happy medium in judging minimum loss from immaturity and the ultimate loss of his entire crop. The leaves of the vines will generally turn brown when they are about ready to harvest. Bush beans can be pulled and stacked in the garden to dry. If the weather is fair, they can be piled on stakes until drying is complete. The stacks must be loose enough to allow circulation and high enough off the ground to prevent rotting. Pole beans can be left where they grew until dry. If the weather at the time of harvest is damp or frosty, pile the vines on the barn or garage floor under cover until dry.

When the beans have dried (the pods will shatter and the beans will begin to lose their grip), you can either process them immediately or wait until other outside chores are wrapped up for the winter.

Small amounts of beans can be shelled by hand. If you have a large harvest, you will find it more efficient either to flail the bean pods or use a hand- or power-operated winnowing machine (the kind you often see housing petunias on rural lawns).

When farmers had commodious barns, come early fall they would sweep the central aisle, distribute the bean pods in a neat windrow along its length, and go to it with the flail. This was a farm chore young boys were encouraged to practice, for it allowed them to vent their aggressions in a positive, family way. When all the pods had been beaten effectively, they were raked away, and what was left was swept up and deposited in baskets. The sliding doors at both ends of the barn were pushed open to create a proper draft, and the harvesters turned their beans from the baskets through wire sieves into barrels. What chaff did not blow away was caught in the sieve and shaken out. The beans, now clean, were stored away to use either for eating or next year's seeds. Flailing can be done on a lawn by spreading the beans on a canvas or sheet, but the weather must be dry with a fair wind blowing.

A small winnowing machine will do the same job by creating a forced draft through oscillating wire trays as the handle is turned. The chaff is blown away and the bean seeds shaken down to a waiting receptacle. Working models of these once common time-savers are being collected by antique buffs rather than by homesteaders.

Winnowing machine

Beans growing are subject to attack by beetles, rust, mosaic, and woodchucks; dried, they may be permeated by weevils. These parasites lay their eggs on the green pods while the beans are in the garden. They hatch into grubs, which burrow through the pod into the bean. Several hatchings may occur while the beans are in storage. To combat this infestation, after drying, place the beans on screened trays in a cold oven. Heat gradually to 135° F and hold for thirty minutes. Cool before storing. Store dried beans in air-tight tin or glass containers in a dry, cool place (45° to 60° F).

There are many ways to use your harvest in cooking. Dried beans must either be soaked overnight or parboiled before they are ready to cook. If time is essential, and you have neglected to soak the beans, cover them with cold water, bring to a boil, and boil for one minute. Remove from heat, cover, and allow to sit forty-five minutes to an hour. Finally, drain and rinse in cold water. Now they are ready to cook.

Baked Beans
(10 to 12 servings)

Each family seems to have the one and only recipe for this traditional Saturday night supper. Here is one that is worth trying: Soak overnight or precook two pounds (4 cups) white beans (soldier, Great Northern, or navy pea beans). Drain and put in kettle with cold water to cover. Bring to a boil and simmer gently until partially cooked. Test this by taking a few beans on the tip of a spoon and blowing on them. If the skins burst, they are ready to use. Drain. Save the liquid. Cut a ½-pound piece of salt pork in half and score by making cuts ½ inch deep. Place one piece in the bottom of a bean pot. Cover with a layer of beans. Coarsely chop two onions and combine with chopped parsley and ½ teaspoon dried thyme leaves (or 1 teaspoon fresh). Spoon some of this mixture over the beans, add another layer of beans, and repeat layering until mixture is used up. End with remaining beans and top with salt pork. Add to reserved bean liquid 2 teaspoons powdered mustard, 1 scant teaspoon ginger, 1 teaspoon salt and some pepper, ¼ cup molasses, ¼ cup brown sugar, and enough hot water to cover beans. Cook covered in 275° oven six to eight hours or until done. Uncover for the last hour.

NAVY BEAN SOUP

Soak overnight or precook 1¼ cups navy beans. Drain and place in kettle with a meaty ham bone, 1 medium onion chopped, 1 sprig savory, 1 bay leaf, 1 scant teaspoon salt, and pepper. Bring to a boil and simmer gently until tender (2 to 3 hours). Remove bay leaf and ham bone. Dice any remaining pieces of ham, and taste for seasoning. Garnish with chopped parsley. If a thicker soup is desired, blend or sieve some of the beans and liquid and return to soup before serving.

THREE-BEAN SALAD

Make bean salad at least twelve hours in advance of serving. Cook until tender 1 cup each of kidney beans, Great Northern or pea beans, pinto or Vermont cranberry. Cool to room temperature and add finely minced onion, ¼ cup minced parsley (minced green and red peppers, chopped celery; chopped hard-boiled egg may also be added). Dress with ½ cup vinegar, ½ cup oil, 1 or 2 cloves of crushed garlic, salt, and pepper. Garnish with chopped fresh parsley, savory or dill, wedges of tomato and hard-boiled egg.

HOT CRANBERRY BEANS

To serve as a vegetable, soak or precook 1½ cups dried cranberry beans. Cover with fresh, cold water and cook until tender over very low heat about ninety minutes. In ½ cup olive oil, sauté until wilted 1 large onion, coarsely chopped, or 3 green onions, chopped. Add to beans. Season with salt and pepper, and garnish with chopped parsley.

CHILI BEAN PIE

Bring 1 cup water to a boil over direct heat in the top of a double boiler. Mix 1 cup yellow cornmeal with 3 cups cold chicken broth (3 bouillon cubes dissolved in 3 cups water) and add to boiling water, stirring until mixture boils. Place over boiling water in bottom of the double boiler, cover, and cook about one-half hour. While this mixture is cooking, sauté in 2 tablespoons oil until wilted: 1 onion, 1 clove garlic, 1 green pepper, all chopped. (If you wish to add meat, brown one pound hamburger also.) Add one can tomatoes, 1 or more cups corn, 2 cups cooked kidney beans, 1 tablespoon or more chili powder, 1 beef bouillon cube, and salt and pepper to taste. Spread the thickened cornmeal over the bottom and sides of a shallow, buttered baking dish as you would a pie crust. Add the bean filling, sprinkle with grated cheese, and bake at 350° for thirty minutes.

CORN

Flint or native corn is best for home-ground cornmeal, but the seed is unfortunately rather difficult to find. Sweet corn can be

*An old-fashioned
husking party*

ground into meal, but this meal is stickier and not as apt to thicken
properly when cooked. Old-fashioned flint corn is thought to have
been inherited from the Indians in colonial times and is still grown
in isolated areas from Rhode Island to Canada. Today most flint
seed corn has been displaced by dent varieties from the midwest,
but it can still be found in country grain stores in northern New
England, in natural food stores that sell whole grains, and among
farmers who habitually save their seed from year to year.

As the name suggests, flint corn is hard when dried. Its kernels
are larger than those of sweet corn and have a rounded rather than
dented top. This variety grows well in the short seasons of northern
New England but is not disease-resistant. Harvesting a sufficient
crop is an annual challenge, which can sometimes pay off. A further
restriction for today's home garden is that it should be planted at
least a quarter mile from other varieties to assure a pure strain
because it is open-pollinated. Flint corn comes in both yellow and
white varieties. Sweet corn has a more distinctive flavor and is
often ground with flint to combine the advantages of both.

Corn is planted either in rows or hills. In an area subject to
winds and sudden storms, the hill method is recommended. The
grouped stalks will help protect one another. Plant five or six seeds
in hills 2½ feet apart and leave the same distance between rows.
Thin to three vigorous plants per hill. As you cultivate, draw loose
soil up around the plants to add support to the shallow root system.

In addition to insect infestation or blight, corn is tyrannized by
bird and beast at both ends of the growing season. Traditionally,
extra seeds are planted in each hill to placate the crows, which will
be among the first scavengers to find your corn patch. Metal mo-
biles, scarecrows, and prayer are about the only deterrents. Repeated plantings will be necessary if the seed keeps disappearing as
soon as it germinates.

If the corn escapes this devastation, it can be subject to a worse predator the night before you intend to harvest your crop: raccoons. They test the maturity of the corn beginning in late summer. When they judge it fully ripe, they call in their relatives and wreak havoc as they gorge themselves. Broken stalks and rubble will be all that is left. Larger plantings to insure some yield seem only to invite more of these bandits.

In former times when raccoons seemed less plentiful (probably because there was more open space on New England hill farms), corn was left on the stalk until the kernels glazed over. Then the stalks were shocked and left in the field to dry. By mid-October they were brought into the barn and neighbors were called in for a husking party. Later the cobs were stored in the crib and ground as needed throughout the winter.

You can still dry corn without a barn. Husk it and lay the cobs on a screened frame elevated from the ground in full sunlight. Turn several times a day. Either cover at night or bring indoors to prevent added moisture. When dry, store in a mouse-proof place.

Or try a method the Indians used to preserve corn. Roast green corn in a slow oven for at least 1 hour. Test for dryness, then strip off the husks and silks and hang the cobs in dry storage. Unless thoroughly dry, corn will have a tendency to mold, so be sure of its condition before storing.

To turn your dried corn into meal, strip the kernels from the cobs with a knife and grind. For information on home grinders, both hand and electric, see p. 142. A blender may be used for corn also, just as for wheat.

Every family has its own favorite recipes for cornmeal (as for beans). Here are some excellent corn meal recipes that are worth trying:

JOHNNYCAKE

Often called "journey cakes" because they could be transported for long distances, these were originally baked on a board beside the open fire. Later they were cooked on an iron griddle either on top of the fire or on a wood cookstove slowly and for a long time without being turned. Now you can bake them quickly in a fairly hot oven.

1 cup yellow cornmeal
¼ cup sugar
½ cup flour
¾ teaspoon salt
½ teaspoon baking soda
1 cup sour milk or buttermilk (sweet milk may be quickly soured by adding 2 tablespoons lemon juice or vinegar per cupful)

Sift the first five ingredients into a bowl and add sour milk or buttermilk. Stir only until just mixed. Pour into a buttered pan approximately 14″ × 10″. Cook fifteen minutes in a 425° F oven or until lightly browned around the edges.

POLENTA—ITALIAN CORNMEAL MUSH

2 cups cold water
2 cups boiling water
1 teaspoon salt
1 cup cornmeal

Mix the cornmeal with the cold water. In the top of a double boiler over direct heat bring the other 2 cups of water to a boil and slowly add the cornmeal mixture, stirring until thoroughly blended. Add the salt and bring to a boil. Place over hot water, cover and cook one hour. Serve with spaghetti sauce, meat sauce, onion gravy or other savory sauce, or with melted butter and Parmesan cheese.

Alternate Method: After cooking, pour into a shallow pan such as a jelly roll pan so that the polenta is about ½ inch deep. Allow to cool until thoroughly set. Cut into squares and fry in butter on a fairly hot griddle until lightly browned. Serve plain with sour cream or tomato sauce. Or place squares on a cookie sheet, brush with butter, sprinkle with Parmesan cheese and cook in a 350° oven until hot and lightly colored.

INDIAN PUDDING

1 quart milk
2 eggs, slightly beaten
½ cup yellow cornmeal
1 teaspoon ginger
½ teaspoon cinnamon
Pinch each of ground cloves and nutmeg
1 teaspoon salt
1 cup dark molasses

Mix the cornmeal with ½ cup milk. Scald the rest of the milk and add the cornmeal mixture to the scalded milk slowly, stirring constantly until smooth. Cook until slightly thickened. Remove the pan from the heat and add the rest of the ingredients. Mix well. Pour into a 1½-quart baking dish, 2 inches deep. Bake at 325° F for about two hours. Serve hot or warm with whipped cream or vanilla ice cream.

Brewing Apple Cider and Vinegar at Home

To make natural apple cider at home today is not difficult; to try to prolong its life by storage presents a greater challenge.

Just before the first real frost, and after the choicest apples have been harvested and stored in the cellar for winter use, the windfalls and culls are collected and sorted. These stubble-spiked and bruised rejects may be less worthy to be eaten out of hand, but can be ground and pressed to make a number of beverages and enough vinegar to last the winter.

Only two pieces of equipment are needed to make apple cider: one device to crush the apples and reduce them to pomace; another to express their juice. These two functions are usually combined in one machine called a cider press, which can be purchased from a commercial supply house, found at country auctions, or improvised with a few stout planks, several timbers, some wooden slats, burlap or cheesecloth and a car jack (see accompanying diagrams).

The commercial press will extract more juice than a homemade one because it can exert greater pressure through a hydraulic ram or mechanical screw-type press. But for home production, a one-horsepower motor can be coupled to the grinder and pressure on the pomace or "cheese" can be applied by using a jack or turning the screws by hand.

Cider apples hereabouts are best from "natural" trees—those unnamed varieties that spring up along fence lines or appear surrounded by second growth in what used to be a pasture. These have

never been sprayed and may not have an attractive appearance in a commercial sense, but their apples will yield abundant juice to be converted into sweet cider. Locally we find the King, Snow Apple, and one that is delightfully called Sheepnose. The Baldwin is a reliable cider apple. So are more familiar varieties such as the Stark, Cortland, Northern Spy, Greening, and Delicious. Crab apples should not be used alone for they are somehow juiceless in bulk, but a few added to the pomace of other varieties will make a tangier cider.

Expect to produce about three gallons of cider from each bushel of apples. You can make cider using one kind of apple for each pressing or from several, mixed indiscriminately. The former alternative is more time-consuming but will allow you to experiment

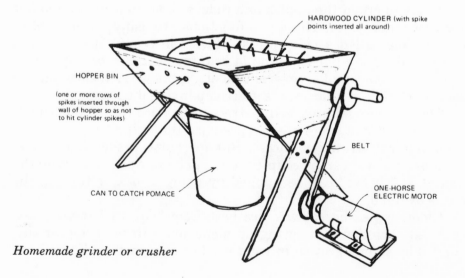

Homemade grinder or crusher

with blending your own cider after the pomace is pressed and the juice put into holding containers.

The New England Farmer of October, 1823, suggests that "the worse an apple is for the table, the fitter it is for cider," and an apple with a tough skin and a yellow flesh will yield a good beverage, generally speaking.

The cooler the weather, the better for making cider—provided it is not so cold as to freeze the fingers or the pomace. Cool weather retards fermentation and the late-season yellow jackets attracted by the cloying sweetness of crushed apples will be less lively.

After collecting the cider apples, wash and sort them, discarding those that are obviously rotten. Grind them (the finer the pomace the greater the amount of juice) and spread the pomace on burlap or muslin on a slatted rack on the press. Leave enough material overhanging to enable this to be folded over the pomace and thereby contain it during the pressing. Add another rack, another layer of material and pomace, etc., until you have a stack of "cheese" layers to fit the vertical dimensions of your press. (Commercial presses are often stacked fourteen layers high.)

Apply pressure slowly. Too quick a pressing will produce a cloudy cider; too much at the wrong time may rupture the fabric surrounding the pomace. (In former times clean rye or wheat straw was used as an encasing material.) The juice must be strained before it is put into storage containers to eliminate obvious impurities.

Sweet cider can be drunk immediately after pressing. But if you intend to store it, you must have clean containers and know how to arrest the fermentation process as the juice passes from the vinous to the acid stage. You may notice this change as some of the sugar changes to starch and a thin layer of bubbles appears on the surface. Soon the delicacy of taste is lost, the head increases, and the cider tastes more tangy. The alcoholic content will rise rapidly and

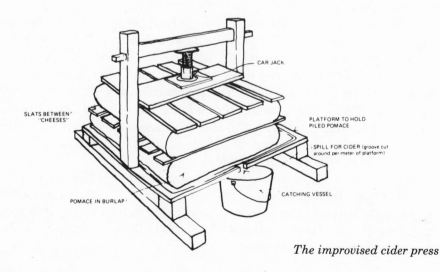

CAR JACK

SLATS BETWEEN "CHEESES"

PLATFORM TO HOLD PILED POMACE

SPILL FOR CIDER (groove cut around perimeter of platform)

POMACE IN BURLAP

CATCHING VESSEL

The improvised cider press

is said to give one a "brainy" feeling. When the alcoholic content reaches its maximum (about 11 percent), another change sets in. This occurs as the acid stage is reached; a "mother" or stringy mass appears on the surface, and the apple juices have changed to vinegar.

Central heating and cement-floored cellars, while making our houses more comfortable and less musty, have eliminated effective storage areas for cider and root crops.

One farm family might consume two or three barrels of cider and vinegar in the course of a winter. Cider was used as a beverage and for cooking. Vinegar was important in treating sunburn and, mixed with honey, to make a tonic. Enameled kitchenware and copper can be cleaned where burned or discolored by rubbing with salt moistened with vinegar. A tablespoonful of vinegar added to the water while cooking tough fowl or meats will save nearly two hours' boiling time. It will also remove lime spots, improve the flavor of stewed prunes, coagulate the albumen when boiling cracked eggs, and help remove lime deposits from the bottom of a teakettle when boiled in the kettle occasionally.

Wooden barrels (thirty-one-and-a-half-gallon capacity) and even hogsheads (two barrels) filled with cider were handy to the cook and thirsty farmhands. Visitors would appear at the drop of a rumor to taste and compare the various stages through which the cider progressed. And young children with a clutch of clean rye straws inserted through the bunghole would be endlessly amused until expressly forbidden their pleasure by stern parents.

Today, glass and plastic jugs can be used for short-term storage. Or cider can be frozen and thawed when wanted. Chemical additives are used commercially and can be in the home to help preserve sweet cider for several weeks. Pasteurization and sealing sweet cider in glass will augment its keeping power but the resulting beverage will be apple juice rather than cider—not the same thing at all to true devotees.

You can refrigerate cider from the press at 32° to 36° F and expect it to last one to two weeks. If you freeze it (fill the container to only 90 percent capacity to allow for expansion), it will keep about one year. Pasteurization requires that the liquid be brought to 170° F and held there for about ten minutes. Then it is bottled, sealed, and will last practically indefinitely. If you are determined to use a chemical additive, purchase potassium sorbate and add one ounce to each two gallons of cider. Mild refrigeration (50° F) will help preserve this for several weeks.

If you can effectively store apples in your cellar and are a devoted sweet cider consumer, the best method of assuring a continuing supply without the worry of having it turn to vinegar is to make cider at intervals throughout the winter in amounts that can be consumed immediately.

But traditionally cider has been stored in stout oak barrels made from heartwood and hooped with metal bands. Barrels formerly used by whiskey makers are popular and available. Make sure your container is sweet-smelling and clean. Use a rinse of soda and water to purify the barrel, or put a pint of unslaked lime in the barrel and add three to four gallons of steaming water. Agitate and let stand until cool. Rinse with cold water and repeat if necessary. "Stumming" barrels was a common practice in the early nineteenth century. This was done by dipping a canvas cloth (12 inches long by 2 inches broad) into melted brimstone. When dry, the canvas "match" was lit and suspended in the bunghole of the barrel and allowed to burn out. This "match" would help suppress improper fermentation and its fumes would be incorporated into any cider left in the barrel. (Additional flavoring could be added by strewing spices like ginger, cloves, cinnamon, etc., on the match before it dried.)

By the 1820s the Shakers, well known for their innovations, found that the slower cider is in fermenting, the better it will be. Modern cider-makers can hold fresh cider twenty-four to seventy-two hours at 40° F to allow the sediment to settle and without danger of too fast a change. Then it is siphoned, tapped, or drained into barrels or jugs. The principal object is to stop the working as soon as the vinous fermentation is complete. Then the vessel is made airtight to prevent the escape of carbonic acid and the intake of oxygen. By mixing the proper quantity of alcohol with the cider at this stage, the Shakers and others stopped cider from turning to vinegar. Although brandy was sometimes used for this purpose, a half-gallon of common whiskey added to a barrel was enough to prevent "souring." Sugar, honey, or molasses were also used, but alcohol was more favored.

CIDER ROYAL was the name applied to a beverage manufactured by the Shakers and made by boiling down fresh cider and reducing it from one-third to one-quarter of its original volume. This was not an everyday drink but reserved for holidays and special guests. It was a richer, more intoxicating beverage, which also had increased keeping powers.

BOILED CIDER was practically the same thing but was not so greatly reduced. This was commonly used for making apple sauce and boiled cider pie. It was also a major ingredient of apple butter.

CIDER WINE can be made by reducing the bulk of fresh cider through the action of severe frost. Fresh cider is poured into wide, shallow vessels and placed where it will freeze. The ice is skimmed off the surface several times a day for two or three days; in this way the water is discarded and the spirits remain. This reduces the original bulk to one-fourth or one-fifth. It can then be bottled and kept at a moderate temperature.

CIDER SPIRIT, another Shaker innovation, was made by distilling the lees, or sediment, and adding one to three gallons of this to fresh cider in the barrel. This was bunged airtight and allowed to stand until mature (usually after the first of the new year).

HARD CIDER can be manufactured from fresh cider rather than let alone to develop at its own rate. Add one-half pound white sugar to a gallon of sweet cider. Throw in a handful of raisins, cinnamon, cloves, nutmeg, ginger, etc., for extra flavor. Bring an air tube tightly fitted to the bunghole to a container of water below. When fermentation ceases (noted by the absence of air bubbles in the water container), the barrel is sealed and stored for about two years. Fermentation in a hogshead takes about eight months. Once hard cider is exposed to air, it turns to vinegar.

APPLEJACK is an alcoholic beverage consisting of the unfrozen core of a container of hard cider.

In dealing with cider vinegar, remember that acid is corrosive. Do not use copper, zinc, iron, or galvanized containers. The interaction of acid with these metals will produce a poison.

One method of making cider vinegar is to leave fresh cider in an open barrel covered with a board or cloth. After the "mother" culture forms, skim the surface before using the liquid. Another method is to add one-quarter pound white sugar to each quart of fresh pressed cider. When cool, add one-quarter cake of yeast and store in a stone or glass jar with only a cloth covering; or plug a glass jar with cotton until after fermentation. In about two weeks, separate the fermented liquid from the sediment and to each quart of liquid add one-half pint of unpasteurized vinegar. Cover with a cloth, stand in a warm place until the vinegar is strong enough to use, then bottle and cork. (Just before bottling you might want to experiment with making different kinds of herb vinegar. This is the time to add sprigs of tarragon, basil, etc.).

With some or all of these by-products of windfalls stored against a long winter, you should begin to experience a feeling of plenty. Here are three more ways to use cider:

APPLE BUTTER

Take pared, cored, and sliced apples and add twice as much boiled cider by measure. Simmer and skim until it is of a marmalade consistency. Sweeten to taste with brown sugar and add spices, if desired. This can be stored in jars or wooden pails practically indefinitely.

Shaker Cider Pie

Put ½ cup boiled cider into a saucepan and add 1 tablespoon butter, 1 cup maple sugar, ¼ cup water, and a dash of salt. Simmer. When slightly cool, add 2 beaten egg yolks and fold in 2 beaten egg whites. Pour into an unbaked pie shell, sprinkle with nutmeg, and bake until the custard is well set and the crust brown.

Apple Mead

For a special beverage, mix fresh apple cider with an equal amount of honey. Stir until dissolved. Pour into a stone crock and cover. Let stand in a warm place for several weeks. Skim when necessary, bottle and seal.

References

"Making and Preserving Apple Cider"—U.S. Department of Agriculture, Farmers' Bulletin No. 2125, available from County Agents, Congressmen, or by writing directly to the Superintendent of Documents, U.S. Printing Office, Washington, D.C. 20402 (enclosing 10¢).

Piercy, Caroline B., *The Shaker Cookbook—Not by Bread Alone—*, Crown Publishers, Inc., New York, 1953.

Any number of household aid or cookbooks published at the turn of the century or before.

Coping with a Whole Pig

Of the several ways of dealing with a whole pig that has been slaughtered and is ready to prepare, the easiest and most dramatic is to serve it young for Christmas dinner, decked out with holiday trimmings. Roast suckling pig is a special treat that predates the omnipresent turkey and even the traditional goose.

A pig on a platter is easy to handle. However, if it has outgrown the oven by several hundred pounds and 4 or 5 feet at this time of year, it will require the efforts of more than one person to turn your assets into a home meat supply that will last part of a year. This can be done by getting a pork chart, assembling some elementary kitchen tools, and reserving a period of uninterrupted time.

If slaughtering anything poses a major problem, get an uninhibited countryman to do it for you. (The majority of providers we know would all be vegetarians if forced to kill their own meat—particularly if it is home grown and has a name.)

PREPARING A SUCKLING PIG

At six weeks a suckling pig will weigh twelve to fifteen pounds and serve eight people. To prepare a small pig for roasting, wash it thoroughly inside and out, giving particular attention to the ears, snout, and feet. Remove the eyes and place a block of wood between the jaws.

Now dry the pig with a clean towel and set it to one side while you concoct your dressing. There are a variety of ways to season and decorate a suckling pig, but because pork is naturally rich in fats, the dressing should not be fancy. Use about one-and-a-half loaves of white bread (one-and-a-half pounds bread crumbs) and mix a seasoned dressing as you would for poultry. One variation could include cooking four large sliced onions in ½ cup butter until tender and golden brown. Add this to the bread crumbs, along with peeled and grated apples, dried sage or savory, and salt and pepper to taste.

Loosely stuff the cavity of the pig until the pig appears naturally plump. Sew or skewer the opening. Place the pig on a large baking pan or roaster, with the front legs folded under and tied in a kneeling position. Add 1 cup cold water to the pan. (You can encase the ears and tail in foil to prevent scorching.) Season well with salt and rub or brush the pig liberally with melted butter or olive oil. Then cover the whole pig with buttered paper.

Bake in a moderately slow oven (325° F) and baste frequently with drippings for three and one-half to four hours (twenty-five to thirty minutes per pound), or until tender when tested with a fork. If by chance the skin becomes brittle during cooking, rub it with a clean cloth dipped in melted butter and replace the buttered paper with a fresh one, butter side down.

Remove the foil from the ears and tail during the last half-hour of cooking. When done, place the roasted pig on a hot platter or cutting board, untie the legs and replace the wooden block with a polished red apple or half a lime or lemon. Insert cranberries, cherries or green grapes in the eye sockets and make a garland of parsley or mistletoe for the neck. Set off your pig with a bed of parsley or watercress. (Some insist that a browned and golden pig is enough by itself to whet the Christmas appetite and should not be decked out to look like a clown.) Make a thick gravy with some of the juices and serve separately.

There are two ways to present a suckling pig to your guests: (1) carve it in front of them, or (2) after they have been seated, circle the table with the platter and retire to the kitchen to carve in privacy. The confident carver (1) will begin by making incisions 1 inch apart at right angles to the backbone, then run the carving knife along the backbone and under the meat to loosen it. Or the novice (2) can cut off the head, slit down the back, take off the hams and shoulders, and separate the ribs to expose the dressing.

BUTCHERING A WHOLE PIG: A full-grown pig raised on garden surplus and milk, or bought slaughtered and halved lengthwise in anticipation of a winter's meat supply, poses a different problem—one of greater proportions and more work. The reward of butchering a pig at home is that every scrap can be put to some use.

Slaughtering is traditionally done after cold weather arrives and continues—depending upon the family's needs and supply—until early spring. Although animals can be killed whenever they reach a profitable size regardless of the season, unless you have cooling facilities you had better follow custom because meat, especially pork, deteriorates rapidly when exposed to warm temperatures.

Therefore, hang the split carcass in a shed or garage only just long enough to allow the body heat to escape—twenty-four hours at a temperature of 32° to 40° F. Then start immediately to cut it up. Cooling the carcass will firm the meat and make it more manageable. It will also give you time to assemble your tools and equipment and decide on what kinds of cuts will best suit your family's needs.

The tools you need for home butchering are simple. Have an array of sharp knives and a sharpener handy. Purchase a meat saw (about $5.00 at the local hardware store). Assemble a wooden mallet, meat grinder, butcher's twine and scissors, freezer paper and tape, and a sturdy cutting board.

If you are a purist when it comes to sausages, you will use as casings the pig's intestine, washed, stuffed and tied off in links. Otherwise, you will either have to buy sausage casing and a gun or make your own cloth bags from muslin (cylinders about 12″ long × 3″ in diameter). For curing hams, sides of bacon, and layering salt pork, it is good to have an assortment of stoneware crocks of various sizes. If these are not available, use metal or plastic trashcans lined with two plastic garbage bags. If you are going to smoke your meat, you should already have taken this into consideration, but a smokehouse arrangement can be constructed (see page 37) while the meat cures in the brine.

When all of these considerations have been dealt with and the carcass has cooled, you are ready to move it into the kitchen and start.

There are several ways of approaching a 200- to 300-pound pig once half of it is laid out on the table. Procure a pork chart like the one a professional butcher uses and study the bone structure and possible cuts. Try to get someone with experience to look over your shoulder and offer suggestions as you proceed for the first time. (See the accompanying butcher's chart for a cut-by-cut approach.)

Even a two-hundred-pound pig (live weight) will provide you with approximately fifty-five pounds of hams and shoulder, forty pounds of bacon and loin, and countless other benefits.

Tackle and finish half a pig at a time. Then you can either duplicate your efforts or vary some of the cuts—remedy your mistakes—when you approach the second half. Your initial attempts may not look like those under cellophane in the store downtown, but yearly practice and note-taking will show you how to improve.

Have two large pots ready on the stove to receive the fat, which is to be rendered into lard. Remove the leaf lard first. This lies in flakes in the cavity of the pig's belly covering the loin and can be pulled out in layers. Cut it up and throw it into the pot. Leaf lard is the finest, whitest lard for pastries and can be stored in the refrigerator or sealed in canning jars and kept indefinitely on the pantry shelf.

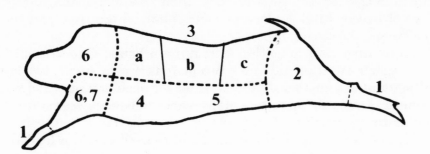

1. *Saw off fore and hind feet.*
2. *Ham: remove ham by sawing hip bone. Trim ham by removing tail bone, hip bone and slip joint.*
3. *Loin: one gigantic whole loin roast or: (a) shoulder chops or shoulder roast; (b) center cut chops, loin roast or crown roast; (c) loin roast or sirloin pork roast, and pork tenderloin or loin chops. (Or Canadian bacon, under spine in cavity, but no roasts then.)*
4. *Spare ribs: saw between second and third ribs.*
5. *Bacon: cut off slabs.*
6. *Shoulder: saw for picnic and butt hams or for whole smoked or fresh shoulder.*
7. *Bacon: take from shoulder bone.*

To minimize waste, always keep a butcher's chart in view while working.

The second pot is reserved for all the rest of the fat (including trimmings from the hams and shoulder) and makes lard for general cooking—or a supply of fat for making soap (see page 181).

As you butcher, divide the cuts of meat into piles depending on their final disposition: those that will be put in a brine or salted down (hams, shoulders, sides of bacon, salt pork, pig's feet); those used fresh or frozen (pork chops, roasts); and those to undergo further processing (sausage meats, head cheese, scrapple). If eating the internal organs (heart, liver, kidneys) does not appeal to you, refrigerate or freeze them, labeled, to provide meals for the dog and cat. Long before the "pigskin" was monopolized by school boys, the washed and inflated pig bladder was being kicked around by farm boys.

After butchering half the carcass, refrigerate what you have done and tackle the other half right away; otherwise, in the heat of the kitchen the meat will become as soft as butter and unworkable.

When all the cutting has been done and lard is simmering on the stove, trim, wrap, and tag meats that are to be frozen in order to clear space for what is to come.

CURING HAMS AND BACONS: When you have trimmed the hams and shoulders of excess fat, dry them off with a towel and weigh them on the bathroom scales. Then rub generously with kitchen salt and let stand overnight in a cold place. In the morning wipe dry and pack them into crocks or plastic containers—hams first, for these will take the longest time to cure, then shoulders, and finally the sides of bacon. Find a place in your cellar where they can remain cool during the curing process.

Now turn your attention to making a brine. One standard recipe suggests eight pounds salt, two pounds brown sugar, two ounces saltpeter, and four to six gallons water for each one hundred pounds of meat. Although there are many variations, this seems to be the maximum proportion of salt one should use. Pour in the brine to cover, and weigh down the meat with a board or plate loaded with bricks or stones. Never allow metal to come in contact with the brine. To prevent spoilage while curing, the meat must be under the brine at all times. If the liquid evaporates appreciably, add more and stir. If it sours, mix a new brine.

Curing time varies according to the thickness of the meat and the amount of salt in the solution. With this brine it will take about nine days to penetrate each inch of meat thickness. Therefore, sides of bacon will be cured before the larger pieces and should be taken out and stored in a cold place until everything is ready to smoke. Some inject brine into hams close to the bone where the meat is most likely to spoil. This is done with a brine pump (like an oversized hypodermic needle) and will hasten the process. Thoroughly dry the meat before smoking (see page 41 for smoking procedure). Some people like to mix a paste of molasses and cracked pepper and rub it into the hams just before smoking.

SAUSAGE

Good sausage is composed of about 25 percent fat. Meat scraps are put through a grinder, seasoned, and stuffed into cylindrical casings. Then they can be frozen. A good country recipe for breakfast sausage is for nine pounds of pork, mix in 2 tablespoons dried, rubbed sage or thyme, ¼ cup salt, 2 tablespoons black pepper, and 1 teaspoon red pepper (optional).

HEADCHEESE

This is a country delicacy much admired by some; for others, the preparation of the head is enough to kill future appetites. If your aim is to use all of the pig, you will have to face the head eventually. To make headcheese, remove the brains, eyes, and snout. Soak the head in cold water to rinse out the blood, then put it in a kettle of fresh water. (Throw in the tail. Not many cooks are ingenious enough to plan a menu around one pig's tail.) Bring to a boil and simmer until the meat falls from the bone. Discard the bone (save the broth for scrapple) and chop up the meat. Add enough liquid to cover, season with salt and pepper, add 1 tablespoon ground mixed herbs, like onion, garlic, and savory. Simmer for one-half hour longer. Pour into a loaf pan, cover with cheesecloth, and weight with a plate or board while chilling overnight. Unmold and slice to serve. (This may be kept frozen up to three months.)

You can also seek out recipes for scrapple (ground bits of cooked meat combined with broth from the headcheese and thickened with cornmeal), pig's feet, tongue, and ears if thrift and specialized taste govern your planning.

One by-product of the pig—and there is a lot of it if the animal has been well fed—essential to enhance the pots of baked beans featured in your winter menus is the meat-laced fat that will become salt pork. To prepare salt pork, cut chunks about 2″ × 4″ and rub generously with salt. Pack into a stoneware crock with a layer of salt between each layer of pork. You can dip into the crock from time to time all winter, but be sure that it is stored in a cool place and well protected from scavengers.

REFERENCE

Wiggington, Eliot, ed. *The Foxfire Book,* Anchor Books, Doubleday and Co. Inc., New York, 1972, pp. 189–207.

Spring Tonic:
Wild Greens and How to Fix Them

If an excuse is needed the first balmy days of spring to get outdoors, what better one exists than foraging for your supper? Melting snows predict the end of winter, but it is the appearance of the first spring greens that finally confirms it.

Traditionally, here in New England, spring greens stimulated the digestion, winter-weary from a steady diet of pies and pork, suet pudding, dried beans and maple sugar. They were also said to purify the blood, combat rheumatism, cure scurvy, gout and ague, and repel kidney stones. We know today—so conscious we are of nutrition—that greens provided essential vitamins and minerals long before they became available year round in capsule form.

Before the garden site is dry enough even to speculate about, there are many wild plants pushing up beyond the doorstep that will satisfy the appetite of both body and soul.

Dandelion greens are among the first that Yankees swear by, come spring. They are preceded slightly by cowslips and mustard greens down in Laidler's swamp, but the ubiquitous dandelion *(Taraxacum officinale)* is everywhere you look. Harvesting first the dandelions that lie close at hand may help rid the lawn of unsightly foliage and blossoms. However, if you want the most rewarding plants, the lawn should be the last resort. It is better to leave that for a weeding session later in the season—or to let the plants blossom and use them to make wine—and to hunt for dandelion greens instead in the fallow garden or along the fence lines.

MILKWEED

DAY LILY

DANDELION

The slightly bitter taste of many wild greens can be minimized by choosing only the youngest and most tender plants. It can also be reduced somewhat by frequent changes of water as the greens cook, but the water-soluble vitamins will go down the drain along with cast-off water.

Many washings are essential before cooking, however, because these greens harbor more grit than most other vegetables. To dig them, use a sharp kitchen knife and separate them from their long taproot. A bit of root attached to the crown (that section of the plant from which roots, leaves, and blossom stems spring) of the dandelion is acceptable. Discard all yellowed leaves and broken stems and any outer leaves that show their age. Wash in three cold-water baths and as many lukewarm rinses. Pause long enough while dunking the greens to allow the dirt to settle to the bottom of the pan before you lift them out.

More greens are needed to satisfy the appetite than you might think. Cooking will reduce their bulk drastically, so be prepared to harvest and clean a monumental pile.

The country way of fixing dandelions is to bring 1½ quarts of water to a rolling boil; enter the greens with cut-up pieces of fat salt pork and simmer them together gently for an hour or more. In the last half-hour before serving, add pieces of peeled potato and finally, after tasting, salt. To serve, lift out the greens and place them in a heated bowl, arrange the potatoes on top, and surround it all by pieces of salt pork.

At this point a true Yankee, always aware of what is good for him, will drink the "pot likker" or cooking water as a tisane, or mild spring tonic, for this is loaded with nutrition.

To cook dandelion greens so as to retain their shape, taste, color and nutrition, prepare them by washing and then cook, using only the water that clings to their leaves as liquid. Scatter salt among the leaves as you put them in the pot, cover, and apply low heat to wilt them slowly down. When their bulk is reduced by half, add a chopped, sautéed garlic clove and the oil (about 3 tablespoons) in which it has been browned. Stir gingerly to avoid tearing the leaves, and continue cooking until they are wilted to the bottom of the pan. Season to taste and serve.

Dandelion greens can be used for salad also. Blanch a few plants by putting inverted flowerpots over them. (If no pots are available, boards or tiles will do.) Blanching reduces their natural bitterness.

To make a wilted dandelion green salad (three to four servings), coarsely shred 1 quart of greens and place them in a large bowl. Cook four strips of bacon, diced; when crisp, remove from the pan. Add 2 teaspoons sugar to the grease, ½ teaspoon salt, a dash of black pepper, ¼ teaspoon dry mustard, and 2 tablespoons vinegar and heat. Stir until the sugar has dissolved. Now pour this mixture over the shredded greens and toss with the bacon bits.

A Shaker Manifesto of the nineteenth century declares, "To make a good salad four persons are wanted: a spendthrift to furnish the oil, a miser to measure the vinegar, a councillor to dole out salt and spices, and a madman to toss it."

So you do not have to cook spring greens at all. Pick a tender harvest of leaves, wash, drain and dry between towels. Chop coarsely and add to a cold salad of beets, beans, carrots and other slightly cooked vegetables that have been dressed with oil and vinegar, seasoned to taste, and allowed to marinate for ten minutes or so. Toss well and serve.

Dandelion buds are good to eat and so are the crowns. These are somehow reminiscent of artichoke hearts if boiled for only three minutes and seasoned with salt and butter. But the amount one has to dig and prepare may be discouraging.

As soon as the dandelion sends up its first bloom stalk, your harvest of that plant is over. Of course you can still make dandelion wine from the blossoms and even continue to dig the roots out of the lawn. When washed, roasted in a slow oven until brown, and freshly ground, the roots make a passable coffee substitute.

A second spring green often sought by Yankees in a rural setting is the fiddlehead. Fiddleheads are ferns—cinnamon *(Osmunda cinnamomea)*, bracken *(Pteridium aquilinum)*, and ostrich *(Matteuccia struthiopteris)*—much fancied by the Orientals and by gourmet Yankees, who buy them as they appear briefly every spring in

At the right stage for picking, the coiled head of the fern looks just like a fiddle or violin, and the stem will be from 2 to 5 inches long.

the city markets. Blessed is he who can recognize the fiddlehead before it uncurls its three-pronged head along stream beds and in open woods. Harvest when 6 to 8 inches tall. Fiddleheads have a delicate taste and should first be washed in salted water, then cooked from three to five minutes or until tender. Serve with butter or mayonnaise, or cool them quickly under cold water and dress with lemon juice and oil.

Day lilies *(Hemerocallis fulva)* come a little later in the spring. Now naturalized along the roadsides or left to decorate deserted farmyards, these orange lilies are so named because each blossom shrivels at day's end. Long before they have reached this stage, they will provide a delicate taste of spring—earlier than and just as welcome as the first asparagus. Cut shoots 6 inches tall directly above the roots. Remove any large leaves. The inner portions can be sliced raw into a salad or prepared like asparagus in a vegetable steamer. If this is not available, after washing, simmer slightly until tender. As a vegetable, day-lily shoots can be enhanced with hollandaise, oil and vinegar or a horseradish dressing. Make the latter by combining ¼ cup whipped cream, ¼ cup mayonnaise, and 1 tablespoon or more grated horseradish.

Later in the season you may want to try eating the buds and blossoms of this orange lily, as they do in China and Japan. Boil them a few minutes, butter, season and serve like fresh green beans. You can also add them to soups and stews, or even dry them in an attic for winter use.

Since spring beckoned you out to forage for new tastes, thoughts of the winter diet from which you've just escaped may come back if you harvest too much of any one plant—or have met with opposition from a member of the family who would prefer vitamins in smaller doses. All these wild greens can be frozen as you freeze summer vegetables and kept for use in the winter months.

The common milkweed *(Asclepias syriaca)* is another offering of spring—a stalwart plant that seems to like attention because it soon shoots up again in clumps when you have thought it was picked out. Milkweed can be consumed at several stages of growth— the shoots, leaves, blossoms and pods. In late spring, the first shoots (cut when 6 to 8 inches tall and still young enough to snap when bent) can be cooked to introduce you to the promise of even better things to come. Cook a pound of shoots, covered, in a little salted water for ten minutes. Then drain and add butter. Serve milkweed shoots like asparagus—plain with salt, pepper and melted butter. Or cover them with mayonnaise or hollandaise and serve on toast.

If they taste bitter, try cooking them in several changes of water. Never start with cold water. This seems to fix the bitterness. Bring a small amount of water to the boil, add the shoots and simmer. Pour out the water once and add more boiling water. Cover and simmer for about ten minutes or until tender.

The hearty milkweed grows along the roadside, in waste places, and in fallow ground and pastures. The wind-blown seeds parachute to more receptive ground and redistribute their potential every fall. It will often pop up among the cultivated vegetables and provide a welcome taste you have not bent your back to plant.

In addition to these yearly Yankee standbys, there is a host of other wild spring greens for those who yearn to search them out. Foremost is the neglected stinging nettle *(Urtica dioica)* so popular in Europe. Tradition says you will be beautiful if you eat nettles in the spring. Wear gloves while harvesting; the sting of nettles will cause discomfort and may be followed by a red rash. Harvest shoots when they are 3 inches tall, young, fresh, and pale green. Wash in salted water and chop coarsely. For nettle soup, boil your harvest in beef stock, add pearl barley and season. As a vegetable, simmer nettles in a small amount of water, chop or rub through a sieve, add butter, seasoning and serve.

Another way to prepare nettles is to cook, drain and chop them fine. Melt 2 tablespoons butter, stir with 2 tablespoons flour. Add 1 cup milk and heat until thick. Season with salt, pepper and dash of nutmeg. Add to this mixture the chopped nettles and reheat. Thin with cream if desired. This plant is said to purify the blood.

There are many other spring plants to eat. You may find lamb's quarter *(Chenopodium album),* dock weed *(Rumex crispus),* and such other favorites as sorrel, mustard, upland cress, elder blossom and horseradish tops. Some of these could be cultivated in the garden, and most of them produce a higher level of nutrition than those plants we seed year after year and call vegetables.

REFERENCES

Wiggington, Eliot (ed.), *Foxfire 2,* "Spring Wild Plant Foods," Anchor Books, Doubleday, New York, 1973.
Gibbons, Euell, *Stalking the Wild Asparagus,* McKay, 1962.
Wilder, Walter B., *Bounty of the Wayside,* Doubleday Doran, 1943.

Arts & Crafts

Creating Natural Dyes from Common Plants

The terms "spinster," "the distaff side" "warp and woof" and "shuttle" have been woven into our language. So have "dyed-in-the-wool" and "he's true blue." Today, as long ago, the steady rhythm of the spinning wheel and the thump of the loom are heard in homes throughout New England. Weavers and spinsters are doing more of their own dyeing. It's not hard—you can find dye colors in many common plants.

To begin a project in home dyeing, you need a safe source of heat, scales, some pots, a few mordants, a liberal supply of soft water, wool (for this takes the dye more easily than cotton or linen fibers), and plant material: goldenrod, lily-of-the-valley, privet, sumac, marigolds (*tagetes* variety), onions, dahlias, or the barks and nuts of native trees, which abound along the roadsides and in the garden. Do not use beets and other vegetables that produce exotic colors while cooking; these are stains and will quickly fade.

The time of harvest (for most plants, just before they come into bloom), soil conditions, and weather all affect the color of the dye. Therefore, if you plan to dye a large amount of wool the same color, collect more material than you think you'll possibly need from the same place, at the same time, and dye all the wool at once. Harvest plants of different kinds throughout the growing season; use them fresh or label and dry them so you can continue to dye during the winter months.

Natural wool can be purchased as fleece or skeins. When buy-

COURTESY OF THE FRIENDLY FARM

LEFT: *Sorting fleece before washing.* RIGHT: *Washed fleece drying on the line and on the lawn.*

ing skeins, make sure they are not a blend of wool and man-made fibers. (The latter will not take dye evenly.) An unwashed fleece must be soaked twelve hours in very hot water. Then squeeze it out gently—never twist or wring—and wash it in a weak solution of soap. Rinse several times with hot water and spread out in a shady place to dry.

Pots should be of enamel, glass or stainless steel. You will need one large enough to hold four to four-and-one-half gallons of water. Because of the interaction of chemical mordants with the metal, aluminum must be avoided. Iron pots gray or "sadden" colors, but it is possible to use an iron dye pot instead of adding ferrous sulphate (see below).

You should have a scale that will measure in fractions of ounces up to a pound. (It takes about one and a half pounds of wool to make a man's home-knit sweater.) Use a postal scale to measure the one-sixteenth of an ounce of chemical mordants sometimes required.

Mordants make it easier for the dye to unite with the fiber by forming a chemical bridge, which will fix it permanently. Although some plant material can be used without a mordant, most require one. Historically, vinegar, ammonia and caustic soda were commonly used. To produce a wider range of colors today, you should have on hand cream of tartar (potassium acid tartrate), alum (potassium aluminum sulfate), chrome (potassium dichromate), tin (stannous chloride), and iron (ferrous sulphate). Purchase these from your druggist or from a dye and chemical supply house. Alum/cream of tartar is the most commonly used mordant. It brings out the soft, natural colors of the dyes. Chrome will make the colors more authoritative; tin brightens them, and iron "saddens" or grays them.

To mordant with alum, heat four to four-and-one-half gallons of water. Dissolve four ounces alum and one ounce cream of tartar in a small amount of water. Then add it to the pot. Immerse one pound wetted, clean wool in the bath and simmer for an hour, stirring the wool occasionally. Lift out the wool and press gently to remove water. Rinsing is not essential unless the wool feels sticky, in which case you have used too much alum. Adjust the amount for the next bath. The wool is now ready for the dye bath.

It is possible to mordant wool with chrome, tin or iron (use one-half ounce of the chemical for one pound of wool) as you would with alum/cream of tartar. However, tin sometimes causes the wool to become brittle. Chrome is light-sensitive, so wool pretreated with this mordant will have to be protected from light until the dyeing has been completed. It is better to add chrome, tin or iron as desired to alum-mordanted wool in the final minutes of the dyeing process. The wool must be lifted out and set aside while the chemical is being dissolved in the dye bath. (See directions that follow for specific amounts.)

Use wooden spoons, glass rods or smooth sticks to stir the wool. Keep all dyeing utensils and chemicals isolated from cooking equipment and out of reach of children.

Dye plants growing in New England will generally yield soft earth colors ranging from yellows through golds, greens, reds, tans, and browns to grays. They can be divided into two groups according to how they are prepared: the leaves, stems, flowers or skins of common plants, together with barks, nuts or roots, form the "fresh" group; and lichens—parasitic, flat growths that appear on rock out-

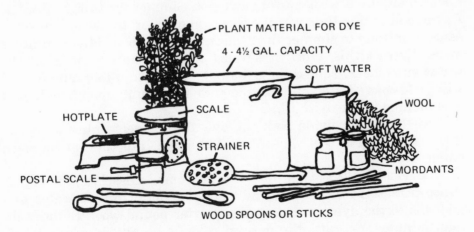

Have everything on hand before beginning the actual dyeing.

croppings in the higher altitudes of New England—form the "fermented" group.

Plant material can be used either fresh or dried. You need about one peck (2 gallons) of stems and leaves or blossoms; one pound of nut shells; or one-half pound of roots for each pound of wool to be dyed. Dried plants can be broken and pulverized; fresh material should be shredded with a sharp knife or scissors before trying to extract the colors.

Crumble or chop the material into pieces, cover with water, and let stand overnight. In the morning bring to a boil and simmer for at least one-half hour to release the entire potential. Add enough water to cover the wool (about four gallons). *The addition of water will not dilute the dye. Once the potential has been released, it will always be available regardless of the volume of water in the dye pot.* Now heat the dye before adding wetted, alum-mordanted wool. Enter all the wool at once so the lot will dye evenly.

Directions for a specific experiment with onion-skin dye follow. You should obtain four different colors from the same dye by changing the mordant. Your colors will range from golden yellow to mossy green.

Place the dry outer skins of common cooking onions in the pot and cover them with water. Let stand overnight. You will need about ten ounces of skins to dye one pound of wool, but you may reduce the amounts proportionally. (One way to collect enough of this material is to ask your grocer to save skins for you from the bottom of his bins.) In the morning, boil the mixture for at least one-half hour. If you are dyeing fleece, enclose the dyeing material in cheesecloth and leave it in the dye pot: if skeins, omit the cheesecloth. You can shake the wool after dyeing it, and the onion skins will drop off. Add enough water to make four to four-and-one-half gallons.

YELLOW—OLD GOLD: Enter one pound of wet, alum/cream of tartar mordanted wool into the dye pot. Simmer for thirty minutes. At the end of this time remove three-quarters of the wool and set it aside. Continue to simmer the remaining wool about fifteen minutes more. Extract this, rinse it several times in hot water until the water runs clear, squeeze and hang to dry. Alum-mordanted wool will yield colors from yellow to old gold, depending upon how long it is simmered in the dye bath.

At this point divide both the dye and the remaining wool into three equal parts. Put one-third of the dye into the pot for each batch.

COPPER—BURNT ORANGE: Use chrome. Dissolve one-eighth ounce potassium dichromate in a small amount of hot water and add this to the dye pot. Enter one-quarter pound wool. Simmer fifteen minutes, or until the desired color is obtained; take out the wool, rinse it thoroughly in hot water, squeeze, and hang up to dry in a shady place.

Mossy Green—Saddened Khaki: Use iron. Follow the same procedure you used with the chrome. Remember to clean the pot thoroughly after you have discarded the used dye, for you do not want any residual chemical to affect the next lot.

Bright Orange: Use tin. As above.

Each of your wool-dyeing experiments should be labeled immediately with a notation made of the mordant, date and dye material to avoid later confusion and to enable you to duplicate a specific color.

The procedure is the same for other common plants. Among these are: marigold blossoms (*tagetes* variety) for yellow, buff and old gold; spring leaves of lily-of-the-valley, greenish-yellow; privet leaves, yellow and gold; goldenrod, golds and tans; dahlia blossoms, rosy reds; coreopsis, yellows and burnt orange; bracken, soft greens; and Lombardy poplar leaves for lime yellows and golden browns.

Roots, barks and hulls from nuts of native trees often contain tannic acid. This is a natural mordant, but without additional chemicals the colors will tend toward the dark side and fading can occur. The basic procedure for dyeing is the same as above. However, the amount of soaking required to release the dye depends on the freshness of the material. If fresh, soak overnight and boil for two hours; if old, the material should be soaked for about a week. You can easily tell when the water starts to pick up the dye color.

The inner bark of common trees should be gathered in the spring when the sap is in the trees. If used dried, bark can be pulverized; if fresh, it should be finely chopped. A dye made from white birch bark will yield light browns. Other commonly used barks are apple (yellow-green), black willow (rose-tans with alum), spruce (tans), and black walnut (browns).

Other colors can be obtained from wood chips. Keep them separated according to tree variety and experiment for colors.

Gather butternuts in the fall while still green. Remove the hulls with a hammer (save the nut meats for the cook) and soak them. For dark tan: after thirty minutes of simmering, remove the wool, dissolve one-sixth ounce iron in the bath. Reenter the wool and simmer with the hulls until the desired color is reached.

Cut eight ounces of fresh bloodroot into small pieces and soak them overnight in a pot of water. Alum-mordanted wool in this dye bath will be colored a number of soft reds.

The other way of extracting dyes at home is through fermentation. For this you can use lichen. Two varieties of this parasitic plant are native to New England: *Umbellicaria pustula* and *Gyrophora dillenti*. These are potent dyes (dark reds and purple blues), which can be used over and over again without appreciably exhausting their strength for as many as ten dye lots. No mordant is necessary. They can also be used as a cold-water dye bath by simply submerging wetted wool overnight in the dye once it has been properly fermented.

Lichens grow on exposed and eroded rocks at high altitudes. They prefer moist conditions and appear to be leatherlike green or olive plaques with dark brown or tan undersides. Lichens are most easily harvested when water-soaked.

Collect lichen in August and allow it to dry thoroughly. When ready to use, pulverize the plant material by rubbing it between your hands or putting it through a sieve. Place it in a wide-mouthed gallon jar with a close-fitting lid. Moisten the lichen and slowly add a solution of 1 part ammonia (nonsudsing kind) to 2 parts of water. Cap and shake vigorously. Keep it in a consistently warm place between 60° F and 75° F for a period of fifteen to twenty-eight days. Shake the jar every two or three days.

When ready to dye, enter wool in a cold dye bath and leave overnight. This results in a magenta or "bishop's purple." Dyeing can be repeated each night until the bath seems exhausted. But to get even more mileage from this material, heat it in an enamel pot and let it simmer five to ten minutes. Enter wetted wool now and successive dyeings will produce brilliant orchid colors. When this seems to have finished off the dye, add a small amount of vinegar and enter more wool for rosy tans.

You can also grow your own dye herbs: try weld (greens and yellows), Our Lady's bedstraw roots (coral reds), wild marjoram (violets), and dyer's camomile (yellows). (See Richard M. Bacon, *The Forgotten Art of Growing, Gardening and Cooking with Herbs,* Yankee, Inc., New Hampshire, 1972.)

Because a competent teacher can save you endless hours of frustration, join a dyer's workshop if there is one in your area.

References

Adrosko, Rita, *Natural Dyes and Home Dyeing,* Dover Press, New York, NY 1971.

Bolton, Eileen M., "Lichens for Vegetable Dyeing" (obtainable from Robin and Russ Handweavers, McMinnville, Oregon 97128, or Earth Guild, 149 Putnam Ave., Cambridge, MA 02139).

Davidson, Mary Frances, *The Dye-Pot,* Rt. 1, Gatlinburg, TE 37738.

Krochmal, Arnold, and Connie, *The Complete Illustrated Book of Dyes from Natural Sources,* Doubleday & Co., New York, NY 1974.

Castino, Ruth A., and Marjorie Pickens, *Spinning and Dyeing the Natural Way,* Van Nostrand Reinhold Co., New York, NY 1974.

"Dye Plants and Dyeing—A Handbook," Brooklyn Botanic Garden, Brooklyn, NY 11225.

"Natural Plant Dyeing—A Handbook," Brooklyn Botanic Garden, Brooklyn, NY 11225.

Making Plain and Fancy Soap

About 60 percent of the world's supply of soap is consumed in this country. This reflects our passion for cleanliness as a result of the marriage, more than a century ago, of soap manufacturers and the fledgling advertising industry.

The two basic ingredients of soap are lye and fat. Lye can be manufactured at home by dripping water through wood ashes in an ash pit or open-ended barrel. Or you can purchase commercial lye in the local supermarket. Animal fats saved from cooking or home butchering or bought from your meat man all make good soap. Vegetable oils (olive, linseed, coconut, etc.) are becoming common in natural food stores, and vegetable shortenings (Crisco, Spry, *et al.*) have been available at grocery stores for years.

In the horse-and-buggy era of a hundred years ago soap was soap, without fancy frills. Its color varied from pale yellow to tan, largely depending on the age of the fats used. It smelled like soap, with a slight overtone of fat, and it performed with a vengeance when used to scrub clothes and wash dishes. Sometimes the housewife would make a smaller batch of scented soap (using herbal decoctions like lemon, lavender, or rosemary) for the washbasin in the guest room or to caress more tender skin. Yet it was the homemade bar soap that she depended on.

Soap-making usually took all day and had to be done outdoors in a large kettle, sometime after butchering and before the weather warmed. Wood ashes were collected from stoves and fireplaces and

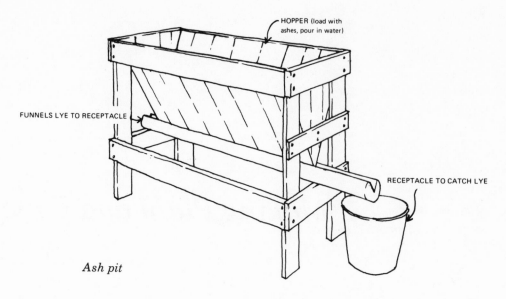

HOPPER (load with ashes, pour in water)

FUNNELS LYE TO RECEPTACLE

RECEPTACLE TO CATCH LYE

Ash pit

dumped into the ash pit. This might be simply an open-ended barrel set on a slanting board. More often it was an ash pit specifically constructed for lye-making. Made of stout oak planks, it was built in a "v" shape some 5 to 6 feet long and about 4 feet high, with a trough (made by nailing two 6-foot boards together in a "v" form) along the bottom to channel the lye and lead it to a holding receptacle (see diagram). Straw lined the bottom of the pit to prevent the ashes from seeping through. With the ashes loaded, water was poured in from the top, and when it had trickled through as lye and was stored in a stone crock or wooden barrel, one of the ingredients for making soap was ready. Chemists know this product as potassium hydroxide or caustic potash.

Meanwhile, animal fats (bacon drippings, pork rind, suet and trimmings from late fall butchering) had all been hoarded for the annual soap-making day. Beef fat (tallow) is still the principal animal fat used and will produce the hardest soap. But mutton fat, pork fat (lard), and even goat fat were all commonly used. The fat was thrown into the iron kettle over a brisk fire outdoors and rendered (reduced to liquid form by melting).

Then the lye was added, and the whole mess stirred until it acquired the consistency of honey or jelly. The soap was poured into molds or flat trays and allowed to harden and age.

Soft soap was made by stopping the boiling process early. The soap was stored in stone crocks or barrels in the cellar and dipped out when needed for laundry. Often a small wooden bucket of soft soap (or a coconut hull with the top cut off) was left near the kitchen sink for doing the dishes. This was a liquid soap long before the days of the ubiquitous plastic squeeze bottle—fierce stuff on both hands and clothes—but effective.

To render fat safely in the kitchen today, the fat should be first finely divided, preferably by putting it through a meat grinder, then placed in a rather flat pan, and put in a moderately warm oven (250° F to 300° F, no higher). The entire rendering should take no more than half-an-hour. The liquid fat can be poured off every ten minutes or so to make it easy to handle. Not all of the fat will render, and what doesn't is called "cracklings" and can be nibbled, used to make crackling bread, squeezed out or discarded. Strain the liquid fat through several layers of cheesecloth to remove any impurities.

Lard and tallow will keep nearly indefinitely if refrigerated or sealed in a canning jar and stored in the cellar. Or you can make your soap the same day you render the fat.

When the lye is ready and the fat rendered, you are ready to begin. Commercial lye (sodium lye or caustic soda) can be bought under various labels at the grocery store. Be sure to buy *flake* lye, not one of the by-products.

Use only enamel or stainless steel containers when working with lye. Chemical reactions will cause aluminum, tin, or iron pots to corrode or rust. Stirrers should be either glass or wooden. Protect your hands with rubber gloves.

In making soap with homemade lye, you will find some recipes merely state to combine the two principal ingredients. This means to add the lye to the fat. The measure of success depends on the slowness of the combining and the temperature of each ingredient (between 90° and 98° F). Women who have been making homemade soap all their lives feel the outsides of the containers as a way of testing the temperatures. Then they can heat or cool either one accordingly. Lacking such experience, use a thermometer until you get the hang of it.

The use of commercial lye, a potentially dangerous substance, requires temperature control for safe and successful results. The directions on the can of one popular brand of flake lye spells out the fat/lye temperatures specifically:

Sweet lard or soft fat: 85° F—lye solution at 75° F
Half lard, half tallow: 110°—lye solution at 85° F
All tallow: 130° F—lye solution at 95° F

Always add the lye to the fat in a thin, slow stream, stirring constantly. Otherwise, "No Soap"—an expression of negation, which came from seeing the mess either curdle or refuse to jell. Stir slowly for ten to twenty minutes until the mixture is as thick as honey. Then pour it into molds.

Here is one way of making a hard, white soap:

The ingredients are six and one-half pounds of rendered fat, one can of commercial lye, and ½ cup sugar, which makes the soap lather. (In former times small amounts of borax, kerosene and ammonia were all added to increase the cleansing power of the soap.)

Clarify the fat by boiling it with an equal or larger amount of water in a large pail or stock pot. This will remove the salt and other impurities. Pour off the fat and discard the sediment.

Dissolve sugar in 1 cup very hot water. Add this to 4 cups warm water. Now empty a can of lye slowly into the mixture and stir. The lye will heat up on contact with the water. Since it will cause fumes, this should be done either *outdoors* or in a *well ventilated* kitchen. It is also a good precaution to have a glass of water and vinegar on hand to sip to stop coughing, or, should some splatter on your skin, to bathe the irritated area. *Keep lye out of reach of children;* caustic soda can be fatal if swallowed.

As the temperature of the lye mixture reaches that specified, pour it into the fat in a fine stream, stirring constantly. When the mixture approximates the consistency of honey, pour the liquid soap into a shallow pan or cardboard box (like a shoebox) that has been lined with a cloth wrung out in cold water. Score the soap with a knife when slightly hardened. When set, cut into squares, remove the soap from the mold and store.

You can double or triple your ingredients depending on how much soap you want to make in one batch.

Some home soap-makers cover the molded soap with layers of blanket to help control the cooling and hardening process. Others find it just as effective to slide the newly made soap under the wood stove. When blanket layers are used, the soap may take several days or weeks to harden. Under the stove, soap made one day should be ready to use or store the following evening.

Mrs. E. A. Howland, writing in *The American Economical Housekeeper* in 1852, suggests collecting ten pounds of potash and twenty pounds of grease. Clarify the grease. Then put one pail of soft water into the potash and let it stand about one-and-one-half hours. Strain the hot grease into the potash, stirring well and often. More potash will make the soap stronger. If too strong, temper it with soft water before it jells.

You can make saddle soap by using 6 cups tallow, 1 cup lye and 2½ cups water. Heat the tallow to 130° F. Dissolve the lye and cool it to lukewarm. Combine tallow and lye. Stir. Just before molding, add 1 cup glycerine to enrich the mixture.

Try making a luxury soap like the following. You will need one pound of canned shortening, 1 cup pure olive oil, one cup peanut oil, ½ cup plus 2 tablespoons lye, 1⅓ cups water and 3 tablespoons scented oil (see: *The Forgotten Art of Growing, Gardening, and Cooking with Herbs,* by R. M. Bacon, Yankee, 1972, p. 100.). Combine the lye and water. Melt the shortening. Add the olive oil to the shortening first, then the peanut oil. Now add the scent and stir. When both the lye and the oils reach 90° F, combine them and stir until thick. Pour into molds.

Molds for soap bars can be cardboard or wooden boxes, or you

Homemade soap shapes

can work your soap into round balls before it has completely hardened. If you are searching for other shapes for your finished "best" soap, try a variety of plastic molds such as Styrofoam plastic egg cartons, plastic cookie cutters or trays, or make your own disposable plaster of paris molds. Be sure to rub plaster or plastic molds with mineral oil to facilitate getting the soap out, or tear off the mold to expose the finished product.

If you settle for rectangular bars of homemade soap, you can bevel the edges or carve designs on their surfaces after removing them to "pretty them up." Save all the shavings for making soft soap for the bath.

In earlier times color was obtained by using vegetable dyes like beets, spinach and carrots. Blueberries and grapes were also commonly used. Today you can buy small vials of food coloring. Experiment by adding the coloring just before the soap is turned into the mold. (Wavy strips of color can be effected by stirring less or in different directions.)

Adding scent to soap is the real challenge. Natural herbal scents—lavender, rosemary, lemon balm—can be had by steeping plants in boiling water and substituting this amount of liquid in the amount called for in the recipe. (See: *The Forgotten Art of Growing, Gardening and Cooking with Herbs,* by R. M. Bacon, Yankee, 1972, p. 102.)

Essential oils can be purchased from some pharmacies, health food stores, hobby shops, herb shops and perfumery suppliers. These are concentrated fragrances. Candle scents (bought in wafer form) can also be used; dissolve the wafer in the lye.

Some of the most popular scents for special soaps are lavender, lemon, rosemary, rose, jasmine and carnation. Try one of these or make a bouquet using portions of several.

Once you have experience, it will be rewarding to experiment.

REFERENCE

Bramson, A. S., *Soap: Making It, Using It, Enjoying It,* Workman Publishing Co., New York, 1972.

Simple Wooden Toys That Last

Toys have traditionally been made to imitate objects in the adult world. Their success depends on the outlook and skill of the toy maker and the kind of material he is using.

To make a wooden toy, all you need is a saw, a hammer, and a drill. Or you can rely on a sharp penknife and bring back the forgotten art of whittling. To assemble and finish your product, stock up on glue, sandpaper, and a can of boiled linseed oil (or nontoxic paint).

Of course, electrically powered tools will make the job go more quickly. A band saw, jig saw, or saber saw are all useful. A handheld electric drill into which you can also insert a hole-saw attachment, a shaper or sandpaper disc will likewise save time. All of these power tools are relatively inexpensive.

Begin with a home-crafted project that needs a minimum of supplies and equipment. Such a toy might be a climbing bear or a small log cabin.

The bear teaches coordination to the young. It is attached to the ceiling and can reach the top of its climb on parallel cords only if each of these is pulled alternately. When the tension is released, the bear plummets floorward and is stopped by two dowels at the strings' end.

Here are the materials and plans necessary to make the bear (or cat, monkey, or whatever your creative spirit dictates):

- A piece of 1 inch pine board (with or without knots) 8″ × 7″—remember the actual measurement of 1 inch milled board is ¾ inch;
- A 7″ × 1″ × ½″ piece from which the bear hangs (this could be gleaned from salvage if the grain runs lengthwise);
- Three wooden dowels ½″ diameter × ¾″ long, through which you drill a hole from top to bottom;
- Two colored thumbtacks and four carpet tacks for mouth and eyes on each side of the board (or use a knot in the wood for the mouth and drill holes for eyes);
- About 10 feet of Venetian blind cord.

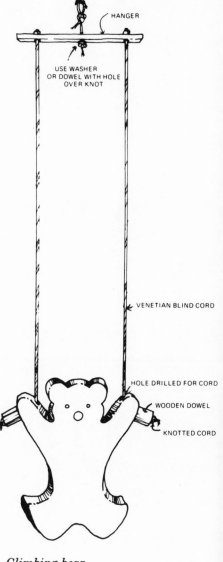

Trace the pattern of the bear on your board, with the grain running vertically, using a piece of carbon paper. Cut around the outline. Drill a hole from the underside of the arm near each hand. Angle the drill about 45° so as just to miss the bear's ears if an imaginary line were extended above his head. Sand smooth and insert or drill the features.

Now drill three holes in the hanger (a 7″ × 1″ piece of wood): one in the exact center through which a looped piece of cord will be inserted to hang it from the ceiling. Thread one of the dowels (or a washer) on the underside to keep the knot from slipping through. Drill the other two holes 1 inch in from each end of the hanger. Cut the cord in half and insert one end through the hole and knot it. Do the same at the other end with the other piece of cord. Make sure these runner strings are knotted on the upper side of the hanger, for these will hang down to the bear; the central loop will extend upward, with the knot and dowel underneath.

Thread the lower ends of the runner cords down through the holes in the bear's arms, then through the pieces of drilled doweling, and finally knot them below the dowel to prevent the whole contraption from slipping to the floor.

Hang it from a ceiling hook and you have about as simple and durable a homemade toy as you can make. (A somewhat proficient eleven-year-old child could construct this for a younger brother or sister in about one hour.)

Try your hand too at whittling a toy log cabin with a hinged roof. You will need a saw, pliers, penknife and glue, or a hammer and a supply of ½ inch wire brads. You will also need a supply of sticks about ½ inch in diameter for "logs," and a board scrap 5½″ × 3″ × ½″ thick for the floor.

Glue or nail two 5½ inch logs along the front and back edges of the pine board so they become a log extension of the floor. Now notch each end of all subsequent logs as you work. Fasten two 4½ inch logs across the ends of the floor so their notched ends are resting on the front and back logs. Proceed as you would in building a

Climbing bear

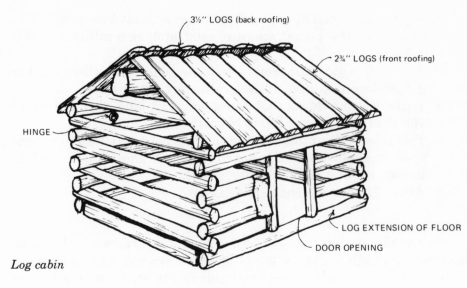

Log cabin

real cabin, alternating working on each side with the proper length logs (5½-inch for the back, 4½-inch for the sides). In the front, leave space to frame a door opening by using four 2-inch logs and anchoring them at the outside corners. To frame the opening and make it stable, split a log 1¾ inches long. Place these vertically, rounded sides inward, and nail or glue them to the exposed ends of the four fronting logs.

When your cabin is four logs high all around, it is time to construct hinges and raise the rafters.

The roof hinges at the back of the cabin. Hinges are made by drilling holes (about 1 inch in from each end) down through two or more of the back logs, inserting a piece of heavy wire and bending over the top of each with pliers, to make loops.

Now for the roof. Three logs 5½ inches long are needed to form horizontal beams: one at the back into which you insert two small screw eyes and through these the loops of the already made hinges; one to rest on the front plate, which extends above the door; and the third to form the ridge pole. Only two logs are needed for the gable ends. These will be 3½ inches long but angled at the ends so as to fit over the rafters and under the ridge pole. When they have been fastened into position, split about five logs 3½ inches long and the same number of 2¾ inch logs. These will be laid flat side down to form the roof. The longer ones are fastened to the back rafter at the lower end and to the ridge pole at the upper end; the shorter ones are fastened to the front rafter and their upper ends are whittled at an angle so as to tuck under the protruding ends of the back roofing.

When you have secured them and tested the roof hinges, you will have made a basic log cabin—a miniature mountain house that will inspire hours of play. If you have more time and material, embellish your cabin with a split log chimney (fixed horizontally to an upright wooden block) and a door on homemade wire hinges.

Try your hand at building a larger structure like a barn or a dollhouse. Take the lead from home crafters of earlier times and you may soon be trying to imitate your surroundings in miniature. You may even tackle building a replica of the house you live in, all scaled down to a child's vision. Get a small one's help to plaster the walls, paint the trim, and construct a miniature brick hearth. After this, of course you will be urged to whittle replica furniture.

Wooden toys endure, and broken parts can easily be replaced at home from scraps of board.

Today's wooden toy makers are producing objects that take advantage of many of the properties of their material; its durability, solidity, and the beauty of grain and feel of wood.

"We're in the fantasy business," Shippen Swift says. He's president of Vermont Wooden Toy Company, Waitsfield. The more than sixty-five kinds of toys his company manufactures from native northern pine and maple are all wood and glue—good examples of the kind of indestructible toy that can be passed on from child to child and from generation to generation. No metal is used (even the wheels of rolling stock are pegged with wooden pins into wooden axles), nor is any paint applied.

Why not paint?

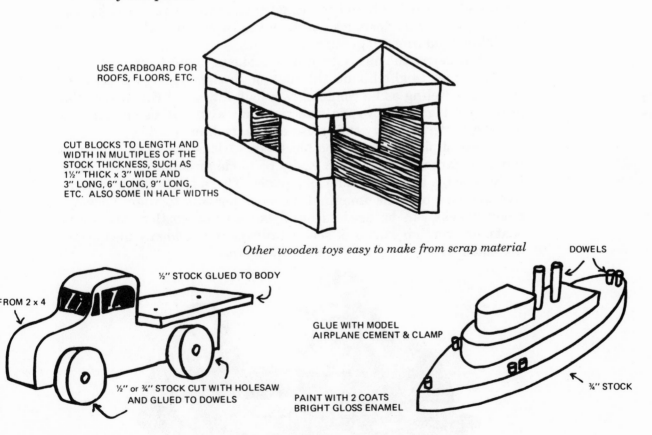

USE CARDBOARD FOR
ROOFS, FLOORS, ETC.

CUT BLOCKS TO LENGTH AND
WIDTH IN MULTIPLES OF THE
STOCK THICKNESS, SUCH AS
1½" THICK x 3" WIDE AND
3" LONG, 6" LONG, 9" LONG,
ETC. ALSO SOME IN HALF WIDTHS

Other wooden toys easy to make from scrap material

DOWELS

½" STOCK GLUED TO BODY

FROM 2 x 4

GLUE WITH MODEL
AIRPLANE CEMENT & CLAMP

½" or ¾" STOCK CUT WITH HOLESAW
AND GLUED TO DOWELS

¾" STOCK

PAINT WITH 2 COATS
BRIGHT GLOSS ENAMEL

The junior partner and plant coordinator, Peter Rogers, quickly says, "Paint can cover a lot of mistakes. Making a toy of wood is still an artful job. Each part must be fitted and glued and sanded perfectly."

It also defeats the purpose of an all-wood toy. It covers the grain.

"Paint adds to the cost, too," adds Donn Springer, an independent toy maker whose workshop is located in the Salmon Falls section of Rollinsford, New Hampshire. He is in his fifth year of producing wooden rolling stock—cars, trailer trucks, and imaginative push toys on wheels.

Springer rarely uses pine, which he maintains is too soft for rigorous use. Instead, he uses maple. This is a hardwood, and the oil finish he hand rubs on all his products brings out the beauty of the grain. He also uses birch veneer plywood from Scandinavia for the bodies of some of his trailer trucks.

For the axles and "hubcaps" of his cars and trucks, Springer prefers metal—sometimes small metal rods with washers and caps, and sometimes pan-head sheet metal screws. He likes the action better than wooden dowel axles and pegged wheels and feels the metal hubs break the monotony of an all-wood appearance.

Most toy makers use white glue (either Elmer's or Franklin Titebond) to hold their products together. This will not color the wood and does not demand the exact temperatures required by liquid hide glue. But Springer points out he would use a water-repellent glue if planning to produce a toy boat.

"Wheels are the hardest thing to make at home," Springer says. The beginner might hit on the idea of sawing through a piece of suitable doweling as he would slice a loaf of bread. "This leaves the grain running in the wrong direction and with any use at all, the wheel would eventually split right across its diameter."

A set of pine or hardwood blocks in various sizes and shapes is the basic fantasy toy and can easily be made at home. All you need is the wood, a saw, and some sandpaper. These allow children creative exercise of their imagination so important to their development. Blocks can be used to build houses and castles, caves and boats, or even labyrinths of secret tunnels and suddenly disappearing floors. True toys generate their own games.

Making Paint from Scratch

Just before the Civil War paint-making shifted from the home to paint factories to supply the burgeoning needs of the urban population. Until then making paint had been the domain of the homesteader, itinerant painters and artists, and carriage makers. As reflected in William Dean Howells's novel of 1885, *The Rise of Silas Lapham*, fortunes were made and lost in early attempts to establish the paint industry.

Few people need to manufacture their own paint today, with commercial mixes available in a wide spectrum of colors. But for special projects, paints made in small batches at home can be economical, authentic, and the start of a challenging avocation.

One reason for reviving this forgotten craft is to obtain an authentic match to an existing color. Few commercial paints will do this. You may need the exact red of an antique bedstead to paint a rail replacement, a batch of yellow ocher to touch up scarred woodwork, or an old blue or green to piece out the side of a cabinet formerly built in. These are problems often encountered by people interested in restoring antique furniture and old houses.

All paint, essentially, consists of pigment (color) and a medium (the vehicle that carries the pigment and dries as a film to help protect the color from outside influences). To these two essentials can be added adhesives, dryers, thinners, varnishes, etc., depending on the kind of paint wanted and the surface to be coated.

Because countrymen were in the habit of using what they had or finding what they needed, they soon discovered ways of bringing color into their lives by painting walls and woodwork, floors and furniture, houses and barns. They even took advice from the Indians who were said to be partial to combining salmon eggs and the bark from the red cedar. Linseed oil and turpentine were usually readily available; milk was on every farm. With combinations of these materials the homesteader either made paint himself or provided soured milk for the purpose to itinerant painters.

As the leading character in Howells' novel found, natural pigments abound in the countryside. Lapham discovered a fine deposit of earth oxides in the back pasture of his father's Vermont farm, and this led him to establish his paint works.

Local clays gave the reds, yellows, and grays so often found painted on early furniture and woodwork. Other natural dyes were used as well. These came from herbs, nuts, berries, tree barks—blacks from carbon, charcoal, and soot.

The combination of milk, pigment, and lime produced milk paint. Its telltale traces can still be found in the corners of antique furniture, around leg turnings and even soaked into the grain of wood unless some overzealous refinisher has worn away the natural patina.

Milk paint is being marketed today by such men as Charles Thibeau of Groton, Massachusetts. As a lifelong lover of antiques and now as a maker of Pilgrim furniture and early wooden toys, he comes by his interest in paint manufacture naturally. By researching old recipes, garnering advice from chemist friends, and constant trial and error, Mr. Thibeau makes and fills mail orders for milk paints in the basement of his home.

"I deal in a specialized market," he says. "People who care for early furniture want it finished authentically. No modern paint will do this." He looks up from mixing one of his own products with a Mixmaster in the kitchen. In the next room his son is painting a reproduction hutch table that, according to the craftsman, will look like an original in fifty years. He quickly adds that to prevent future confusion each piece is branded with his mark.

Most early paints were much stronger-hued originally than they appear today after several centuries of use and abuse. Mr. Thibeau says that most of the pre-1750 furniture that we see in its "natural" state—refinished, rubbed, and polished to show the wood grain—was originally painted to take away the raw look and provide color as soon as the early settlers found the time or could afford the fashion.

Today Mr. Thibeau uses dry ingredients to make paint: powdered milk and pigments, lime, and probably several other essentials, which he will not disclose. This solves the problem of packing, shipping, and ease of mixing and prevents spoilage.

Unless you have a basic knowledge of chemistry or can get the advice of experts, making paint at home is still largely a matter of trial and error. Few manufacturers will tell you their secrets. It is possible to find out the major ingredients but the proportions and the hidden additives which make theirs a distinguished product are closely guarded.

The Shakers, known for their colors as well as the design and construction of their furniture, often stained their products by mixing water with dry pigment, boiling it, and rubbing it on while still hot. To get a smooth surface, they rubbed the wood later with pumice stone and wax.

Lime, pigment, and milk will produce a transparent color, often mistaken for a stain after several centuries of wear. The addition of whiting (Paris white or Spanish white are often mentioned in old recipes) helps make paint more opaque and gives it a better covering quality. This is calcium carbonate—limestone, shells, and tiny marine fossils—that has been washed and finely pulverized. The result of heating or calcining limestone is lime *(calcium oxide)*, also called quicklime, burnt lime, and caustic lime. This was another principal ingredient of milk paints. Often old recipes will call for freshly slaked lime. This is *calcium oxide* to which water has been added. This step in home paint manufacture can be by-passed by purchasing hydrated lime *(calcium hydroxide*—lime that has already been slaked), which is the common agricultural lime.

Lime is an alkali or sweetener; soured milk is an acid. The chemical reaction of these ingredients is important in making a durable paint. They must neutralize each other, so that the combination is neither sweet nor sour. This can be tested in your kitchen by using litmus paper. The paper should not change color when wet with the lime-milk mixture. If the paper turns red, the mixture is too acid (add more lime); if it turns dark blue (too alkaline), add more soured milk.

You should be able to locate earth oxides in your neighborhood. Colored sediments and clay are often found in newly excavated ground, along roadsides and riverbanks, and in gravel pits. Dig them out and purify by adding water and boiling several times. Allow the sediment to form, filter out the impurities, and spread out to dry in a warm place. Then pulverize and store in airtight containers until ready to use.

For those who cannot dig them, dry pigments are stocked by a limited number of paint suppliers. They used to be part of the inventory of every country hardware store, but as ready-mixed and canned paints took over the market, the barrels of dry pigment once available were discarded and never reordered. The Johnson Paint Company, Newbury Street, Boston, Massachusetts, does still carry this kind of stock. There you will find umbers, ochers, siennas, Prussian blue, chrome yellows, Venetian red. Also available are pigments made from exotic imported woods and insects. Another supplier is the New England Resins and Pigments Corporation, Wakefield, Massachusetts.

Milk paints were used recently in re-creating a stenciled room in one of the houses in Old Sturbridge Village. After experimentation with old recipes, the following combination was selected:

> Take a quantity of the curds of freshly skimmed milk [raw and soured]. To this add one-fifth of the volume of the above of freshly slaked lime. Mix together well to form a paste and then add 3 to 5 parts of water. To this now add a sufficient quantity of the desired dry color so that it is of a consistency that will run from the brush.

If a more opaque paint were wanted, another recipe was used, calling for five pounds whiting, two quarts skimmed milk, two ounces fresh slaked lime, and coloring to suit.

If you lack a source of raw milk, you can still duplicate an old-fashioned milk paint using commercial ingredients. To make a colonial red combine one quart buttermilk, ¾ to 1 cup lime, ½ cup raw linseed oil, ground brick dust to suit, and Elmer's glue. The final ingredient, of course, is also a milk product and will give added adhesiveness and body. When applied to a new piece of wood, the paint produces a streaky covering that is properly old looking.

By combining skimmed milk and an oil, as in the following recipe, you can make an interior oil-water paint with good covering qualities:

> one gallon skimmed milk
> 6 ounces lime
> 4 ounces raw linseed oil
> three pounds Spanish whiting (calcium carbonate)
> dry pigment to suit

Besides paint for their furniture and woodwork, countrymen also needed a dependable whitewash to spruce up plastered ceilings and lighten interiors of farm buildings. A recipe book of the past century provides the following "Government Whitewash." It is said to have been used effectively on the east end of the White House for years. You may want to try it:

> Take one-half bushel of unslaked lime, slake it with boiling water, cover during the process to keep in the steam; strain the liquid through a sieve or fine strainer, and add to it a peck of common salt previously dissolved in warm water; add three pounds of ground rice; boil to a thin paste and stir in while hot; add one-half pound Spanish whiting and one pound clean glue previously dissolved by soaking in cold water; add five gallons of hot water to the mixture, stir well and let stand a few days, covered from dirt. It should be applied hot for which purpose it can be kept in a kettle on a portable heater.

References

Andrews, Edward, and Faith, *Shaker Furniture,* Dover Publications, New York, 1950.
Gould, Mary Earle, *Early American Woodenware,* Chas. Tuttle, Rutland, Vt., 1962.
Mayer, Ralph *The Artist's Handbook,* Viking Press, New York, 1970.

Decorating a Wall with Old-Fashioned Stenciling

One way early settlers had of sprucing up the homestead was to stencil a room with repeated geometric patterns in soft colors. This art form was born in the days of the new Republic, bloomed briefly, then perished when it was supplanted by a newer craze—wallpaper. Considered peculiar to New England and often practiced by itinerant craftsmen, wall stenciling had gained spotty acceptance as far west as Ohio and south to the Middle Atlantic states, before its golden age had run its course.

Today, interest in wall stenciling is undergoing a revival. For years art historians have recorded and photographed stenciled walls whenever news of one reached them. Still, much of the work of the early stencilers has been lost, either through neglect or changing fashions. Now, with the pendulum swinging back to individual expression and simplicity, wall stenciling can fill a need because it can be practiced with very little equipment even by those who are not facile artists with a freehand brush.

One modern practitioner of this art is Ruth Wolf of Deering, New Hampshire, a professional stenciler of tinware and furniture, who was captivated by the stenciled walls she found in New England, many painted by wandering craftsmen in the early part of the nineteenth century.

One of the most famous of these craftsmen was Moses Eaton. His stencil kit—discovered in the attic of his house in Hancock, New Hampshire, and now the property of the Society for the Preservation of New England Antiquities in Boston—tells more about the man's techniques than about the man himself. In it are the round, flat-ended stencil brushes he used, dry pigments, and a collection of original stencils he cut, many with the paint still adhering to their surfaces. Comparing these designs with finished walls, it is possible to speculate about both Eaton's work habits and his wandering.

Because few itinerant stencilers signed their work, it is difficult to establish the authenticity of a particular wall. Some stencils were undoubtedly copies by less adept craftsmen; artists may well have exchanged original designs.

Ruth Wolf has spent years tracing and reproducing authentic walls. Today her house, Hayfields,* is decorated with striking patterns, many of which she has reproduced from Moses Eaton's original designs. She has also stenciled the walls of other buildings in diverse parts of New England. One was the White Church in Grafton, Vermont, where from a scaffolding near the ceiling, she restored stencils while the building was being renovated; another was a house newly constructed on Nantucket, which the owners designed as a showplace for their antiques.

The stencil is essentially a mechanical device that allows the reproduction of a pattern over and over and assures more consistency than freehand design. Paint is applied through the cut-outs in the stencil onto the surface beneath. It is the same process packers use today to label boxes and crates.

Unlike the freehand work of the fresco painter, where paint is applied to a wet plaster surface, wall stencils are executed on finished, dry areas of plaster or wood.

Mrs. Wolf was first taken with the simplicity and boldness of stenciled walls. Her years of training as assistant to Esther Stevens Brazer, founder of the Brazer Guild, which encourages the study and practice of stenciling in all its forms, helped her to see many of the problems of stenciling and to master the techniques. As a modern stenciler, she has devised her own methods of dealing with the art. Instead of using stencils made from varnished paper, leather, or tin, the way the early artisans did, she cuts hers from architect's linen. Rather than manufacturing milk paint (see page 192), she buys japan paints which she mixes with alcohol as a medium. A further refinement has been to discard the stubby brushes and substitute squares of velour, which she wraps around her index finger to apply paint through the cut-outs.

To decorate your walls in this way, you will require only a few items, which can be bought at an art supply store: architect's linen, a stencil knife, japan paints in various colors, and alcohol. In addition, you will need some measuring devices: rulers, a plumbline or level to establish verticals, and possibly a chalk line.

---

* *See Yankee* Magazine, Oct. 1968, p. 134.

Most important, you need a blank wall and some idea of how to decorate it.

Finding motifs or patterns to reproduce on your wall will be a challenge. You can trace them from existing walls with tracing paper and transfer the designs to architect's linen before you cut them out. Or you might want to investigate museum collections of stencils. Often organizations such as the Society for the Preservation of New England Antiquities or the State Historical Society in Concord, New Hampshire, will allow you to trace original stencils or have duplicates made. Or, you can design your room around personal themes.

No matter how you decide to lay out your design, you must first prepare a clean wall surface. If wallpaper has been removed, get all the paste off the wall. (If a wet sponge isn't enough, a razorblade will help.) Often you will have to touch up cracks or blemishes if the plaster is old. Stenciling can be done on plasterboard or composition walls if you first give them several coats of oil-base paint. If you wish your designs to appear on a tinted rather than a white background, now is the time to paint the walls a color complementary to the woodwork.

The earliest stenciled walls (late 1700s) probably were only border designs that complemented the architectural detail of the room by outlining the woodwork. If the overmantel was plastered rather than paneled or sheathed, special attention was given it as the focal point of the room. Often early stencilers designed vases of flowers, weeping willows, paired birds, or, more rarely, the spread eagle, symbol of the young nation. Later, probably in the first decade of the nineteenth century, an overall stencil pattern was developed to imitate more closely the imported French wallpapers that were beyond the reach of all but the wealthiest.

Moses Eaton was distinguished for his division of space and use of color. Combinations of soft olive green and brick red marked his work. Often he introduced dark blues, black, and various shades of both pink and yellow to produce decorative patterns.

To divide the space, Eaton commonly stenciled a wide frieze of repeated patterns around the top of the room at ceiling height. He used a baseboard border (or subbase if wainscoting was present) of a different design. The space between was divided into vertical panels by stenciled uprights. Finally, he decorated each panel with alternating motifs or units, some simple and others composite. A composite stencil is one for which two or more stencils have been overlaid to form a single motif. Each stencil introduces a new color and element to the basic design.

Ruth Wolf uses a sharp stencil knife to make the cut-outs. She places the linen on a square of glass, and with one hand cuts the design while the other is free to rotate the stencil when curves are needed. She is also careful to leave a large margin around each

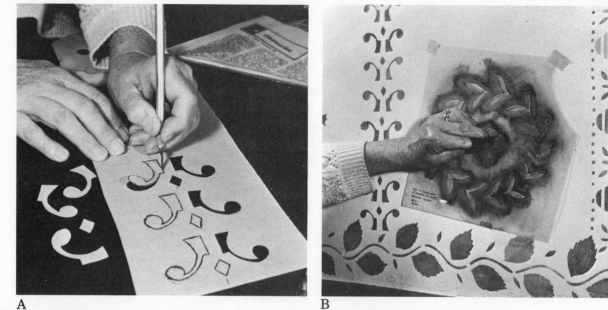

STEPHEN T. WHITNEY

A. *In the stenciling technique developed by Ruth Wolf, the design is first traced or drawn on architect's linen, then cut out with a sharp knife such as an X-acto.*

B. *With the stencil taped in position, the base color paint is applied with a forefinger wrapped in velour.*

C. *The second color or element of a composite design is applied after the first has dried.*

D. *The finished wall—a reproduction of a Moses Eaton design.*

E. *Recently uncovered in a Hillsborough Center, New Hampshire, home, this wall stenciling is thought to be the original work of Moses Eaton.*

stencil, which will help protect the wall while paint is applied. She marks or notches the top and bottom of each stencil so she can align them accurately.

Once a sufficient number of stencils have been cut, you are ready to begin decorating the wall. Lay out the frieze first; then the baseboard stencil.

To apply the paint, Ruth Wolf first dips her velour-covered index finger into a container of alcohol, then into japan color, and finally pats it onto the stencil. Only experience has taught her the proper working consistency of the thinned paint. If it is too thick, the application will be lumpy; if too runny, paint will escape under the surface of the stencil and will have to be corrected. (Let it dry before repainting the background with a freehand brush.) In her method she establishes an immediate contact with the stencil and wall and can control the final results better than with a stencil brush.

"There is a higher concentration of paint where you first touch the wall, less as the paint is used up and before you redip it into the paint pot," she points out.

She prefers this somewhat mottled effect since it softens the motifs and makes them appear more authentic, as though time had already made its mark. Composite stencils are done in stages. The first color is allowed to dry before a second stencil is laid on top of it.

Make sure to clean the backs of the stencils after each motif has been used. Otherwise, you will have to spend time retouching the smudges.

After the job is done, store stencils flat for future reference. Do not varnish or otherwise seal the finished wall. Time will soften the designs and make them look old.

The choice of stencil designs in early days was probably based on personal preference. Although little has been written about the meanings of the motifs, a few have special appeal. The famous pineapple design used by Moses Eaton and copied by others stood for hospitality and often appeared in homes as well as public rooms of taverns. Bows and hearts in the design of a bedroom welcomed a new bride. While these were often combined with a bell, this motif was also associated with the founding of the new Republic and has been found in many tavern ballrooms. The weeping willow, often prominent in the overmantel design, stood for immortality.

The art of wall stenciling was doomed, except in isolated pockets where change was slow, when mass-produced wallpapers became available. Gradually artisans turned to other crafts; the stenciled wall became merely a quaint relic and was covered with more fashionable decoration.

Today several makers of wallpaper are marketing expensive copies of stenciled walls. The cycle has come around to imitating the imitation.

REFERENCES

Little, Nina Fletcher, *American Decorative Wall Painting 1700–1850,* E. P. Dutton, New York, 1972.
Waring, Janet, *Early American Stencils on Walls and Furniture,* Dover Publications, New York, 1937.

Drying Flowers for Winter Bouquets

Take time in the summer and fall to gather and dry plant material for winter bouquets. This was a popular method of bringing color into the house for the long winter months ahead in Colonial times. Today dried flower arrangements can be seen in many historic houses and restored eighteenth-century villages all along the eastern seaboard, for it was an art brought to this country from England where it still flourishes.

Essentially, there are three kinds of dried arrangements. Many people gather and arrange native grasses, fern fronds, interesting seed pods, and fall leaves from the roadsides and deserted meadows. These have been naturally dried and contribute tans, browns, and russet hues to the palette of bouquet material.

Some gardeners raise herbs and everlastings specifically to supply a wider range of more brilliant colors. These types of flowers are harvested at a particular stage of their development, bunched, and hung upside down to air dry. They will keep their natural shape and color for years. Everlastings include such favorites as globe amaranth *(Gomphrena globosa)*, statice *(Statice sinuata)*, strawflowers *(Helichrysum)*, money plant *(Lunaria)*, globe thistle *(Echinops)*, Love-in-a-Mist *(Nigella)*, and the *Helipterums—acroclinium, ammobium,* and *sanfordii*—among others. Herb gardeners can bunch and hang old standbys like tansy and yarrow, wild marjoram, sage and chive blossoms, seed herbs (sweet cicely, dill, coriander), and the perennial favorite, lavender.

A winter bouquet of force-dried flowers.

Air drying plant material is not difficult but a finished arrangement will require a good deal more stock than a fresh one does. Lacking the natural foliage and greenery of fresh flowers, the arranger will have to substitute "filler"—additional material—to fill the spaces between the stems and keep the blossoms where he wants them. Blossoms with their stems should be bunched and suspended overhead so as to allow a free circulation of air around them. The drying room should be protected from direct sunlight—which blanches colors prematurely—well-ventilated, and kept slightly warmer than outdoor temperatures, particularly at night and on damp days. A drying loft or attic is excellent, but even a spare room that can be darkened and freed from normal household traffic will do. If available and safe to use, supplemental heat can be added in the drying room after harvesting everlastings and herbs to speed up the process, but care must be taken not to increase it so much that the flowers become too brittle to work with.

The real challenge in drying flowers for winter arrangements, however, is to force-dry garden blossoms that would only shrivel and fade if hung upside down. This can be done with any of several drying mediums. Force-drying will preserve both the color of outstanding blossoms *and* their natural shapes. When successfully dried and arranged, this kind of special plant material will look as though it had lately been cut from your summer garden no matter what the season.

A winter bouquet, therefore, need not be limited to stalks and pods that Nature alone has dried. It can be arranged with such flowers as peonies, larkspur and delphinium, golden marguerites and daisies, marigolds, zinnias, and roses as well as the more stable everlastings and traditional herb blossoms.

Given the proper conditions and care—protection from direct sunlight and high humidity—the arrangements will last for a year or more. Then, they will gradually fade, lose their brilliance, and eventually become monochromatic but remain interesting.

Quite different from flower *pressing,* a home art much practiced in the Victorian era, the art of flower *drying* is an ancient one. A bouquet of preserved roses was found in the tomb of an Egyptian Pharaoh. Centuries later, in India, the beauty for whom the Taj Mahal was built was also known for her ability to dry roses in sand. Whereas both of these crafts preserve flower colors, the object of force-drying flowers in a medium—rather than pressing them—is to retain their natural shapes, assuring them a third dimension.

The procedure for harvesting flowers that are to be dried differs slightly from that required for fresh flower bouquets. Fresh flowers are cut in the early morning when the dew is still on them or late in the afternoon after the heat of the day. (They can also be harvested during a slight rain to help retain the extra moisture they need.) Flowers destined for drying, however, should be cut only when it is sunny and hot—from late morning to about 3 P.M. This assures that much of the moisture will already have been drawn off by the sun, leaving a minimum amount to be extracted in the drying process. Once flowers have been cut for drying, the process—whether bunching and air-drying or using a medium to preserve individual flowers—should be initiated as soon as possible to best preserve natural color and form.

The oldest medium used for drying flowers is sand. This should be composed of fine, smooth-edged particles made free from foreign matter by rinsing and washing with a detergent. Oolitic sand—whose granules have been coated over the centuries with layers of minerals and limestone deposits—from the great salt flats of Utah is excellent because the particles are naturally round. Don't use common beach sand or sand found in a gravel pit. Its sharp, jagged edges are likely to injure fragile petals during the drying process.

If oolitic sand is not available, you can choose from a number of other mediums.

One is a combination of 2 parts of sand to 1 part borax *or* 6 parts white cornmeal to 1 part borax. In using either of these, you may find that the borax mixture tends to mold in humid weather. In addition, some of the residue of the mixture will adhere to the blossoms and will have to be brushed away gently.

Another absorbent material is commercial cat litter, but this should be used only with the less fragile blossoms and will take longer.

The most effective and foolproof method of drying garden flowers today is to use an expensive but reusable commercial product called *silica gel,* which can be obtained from your local florist. This is a finely granular mixture in which the key crystals tell you when the moisture has been dissipated and the mixture is ready to use. The only loss year after year is caused by spillage. When the silica gel is ready to use, the key crystals will be blue; if they are not, heat the mixture in a low oven (about 150°) until the blue granules reappear. Then allow the gel to cool, and you are ready for the drying.

You should have on hand a supply of tins with lids (fruitcake tins and metal candy boxes do well), a roll of masking tape to seal the lids while the flowers are drying, a supply of freshly harvested flowers, a pair of clippers, and a small spoon.

In all of the drying mediums you can position your flowers in one of three ways: face up, face down, or laterally.

To dry individual blossoms, cut the stem off about an inch below the flower head with the clippers. (Later you will have to tape a false stem to the flower, using either floral wire or discarded stems of goldenrod, tansy, etc.) Do not harvest more flowers than can be arranged in the drying mixture in about fifteen minutes. You should not attempt to dry flowers that have come from a florist or ones that are past their prime. Blossoms for drying must be absolutely fresh, and they should be processed as quickly as possible after cutting.

Only experience will tell you which flowers and what colors will dry most effectively. Large, fleshy blossoms (Oriental poppies, anemones, water lilies) may dry, but the petal structure is such that they will quickly reabsorb moisture when exposed to the air. Yellows and pinks are dependable colors; blues are fairly dependable but may undergo a slight color change. Reds are difficult. Unless you dry a flower that has a good percentage of orange in its makeup, the red will darken to a mahogany, nearly black. Whites, too, often present problems. They may turn a creamy, parchmentlike color.

With your harvest at hand, work quickly and carefully. To dry blossoms face up or face down, put a layer of drying medium about 1 inch deep in the bottom of the tin.

Flowers such as roses and peonies should be dried face up to preserve their natural form. Place the bloom, stem down, in the mixture and allow a 1-inch space all around each so it can expand while drying. Take a handful of the medium and gently trickle it around the edge of the container as far from the blossom as possible. The mixture will flow into the center slowly and cover the lower petals first. Work around each blossom in a circular way so that the level of the medium gets higher and higher. Then with a spoon, slowly sift the medium into the center of the flower, keeping the general level as uniform as possible until none of the flowers can be seen. Level the mixture by tapping the sides of the container, place

". . . a reminder of summer that will last all winter."

the lid on it and tape around the edges to seal. It is a good idea to label the top of each container with the kind of flower and the date the process was begun. This will give you an idea of when to take it out and the approximate timing for similar flowers.

Dry daisy-type flowers face down. You will not use as much of the mixture and more flowers can be dried at the same time. Do not, however, allow any of the petals to touch one another.

Large sprays—delphinium and larkspur, for example—which you want to keep intact should be dried laterally. If you do not have a large enough tin, make a temporary container with heavy duty aluminum foil. Proceed as you would in drying flowers face up.

If you must move your containers after they have been filled, do it gingerly. Flowers can become distorted at this stage by any jiggling.

How long will it take flowers to dry? This knowledge will come by trial and error. If you keep accurate records on the tops of the lids or in a notebook, you will gain experience quickly. Generally, if using silica gel, larkspur will take about four days, daisy-types three to four days, large compact marigolds at least a week or longer. To check their progress, uncover the tin after several days, gently locate and lift out one of the blossoms. If dry, the petals will feel papery and stiff. If left too long, they will shatter. (If you have a particularly fine specimen that you cannot do without, these petals can be glued on again.) If the flower is not dry, gently replace it, seal the tin and wait a few more days.

Even if the blossoms are dry, it is a good idea to uncover them and let them sit on top of the mixture for a few more days. Never uncover newly dried blossoms on humid days; like sponges, they will reabsorb any moisture that is in the air.

Because flowers must be dried while the garden is in bloom, you will have to store your successes until you are ready to make a bouquet for winter. Use a wide-mouthed glass jar with a screw-on lid. First, sprinkle a few spoonfuls of the drying mixture in the bottom of the jar. Then place the blossoms in layers separated by balls of tissue paper. Store in a dry, dark place.

There may be several causes of failure in drying garden flowers. The foremost will be the lack of patience and care during the drying process. Another will be from having harvested your blossoms at the wrong time or under too humid conditions. This can only be corrected with experience. Finally, failure may be caused by selecting varieties of flowers that do not dry successfully.

But given success, you will be able to fill your house with a reminder of summer that will last all winter.

Weaving Baskets with Black Ash

Using his grandfather's tools, wooden forms, and methods, Chet Colburn, Jr., of Weare, New Hampshire, has resurrected the family craft of making baskets with strips of black ash.

There are as many kinds of woven baskets as there are materials and uses. Colburn's father and grandfather, who had been general farmers in southern New Hampshire, specialized in making bushel baskets with handles for carrying or storing apples and potatoes. They also made peck measures, egg baskets, and experimented with a variety of shapes and designs, many of which still hang on display from the beams in the younger Colburn's house.

According to Colburn's father, who has been helping his son reconstruct the family craft, which he learned from *his* father as a boy, they produced about a hundred bushel baskets and several other containers during a winter season.

What makes the Colburn baskets distinctive is that they have a concave base to give the basket stability when it is set on a level surface. Otherwise, loaded either with heavy farm produce or fragile eggs, the basket would have a tendency to tip and spew out its contents.

The baskets are all made from black ash. Locally sometimes called brown or marsh ash, *Fraxinus nigra* is one of the more valuable but elusive members of the prolific ash family. Because this wood splits evenly and bends without losing strength, it has traditionally been used for making baskets, chair bottoms, and barrel hoops. After the leaves have fallen the tree is sometimes confused with a young elm. However, this ash is a slow-growing, slender tree that prefers swampy areas and often flourishes in standing water.

In the fall Colburn locates an ash 8 to 10 inches in diameter. He peels the tree green. Using a lightweight mallet to pound the log with one hand while lifting the peel with the other, he works down the entire length of the log. It is relatively easy to peel off the soft brown wood in annual layers, like lifting off thin sheets of veneer. Ideally, the wider the peel, the better the result. In bigger trees the grain will be thicker and the splits more workable. There is some evidence—both in the memory of the senior Colburn and the width of the grandfather's stripping device—that black ash used to grow larger than it does today.

After peeling the tree, Colburn rolls and bundles the strips and leaves them in a corner of the workshop to dry. Fresh peels will shrink and retain a raw, new look. Just before he starts weaving, Colburn soaks the dried strips in water to make them pliable.

The basic steps in making a basket have not changed over the years. Only the simplest tools are necessary. First, you must split, or "strip," the peels into uniform widths, then weave a base and sides, and finally finish off the rim to give it strength.

To strip the peels, Colburn pulls them through a simple device his grandfather used: essentially, it is a wooden box in the top of which are embedded a row of razor blades at 1-inch intervals. The box is about 6 inches across but could be made to any dimension.

To form the base of the basket, Colburn uses his grandfather's base mold or form. This is a low conical, turned-wood block, which is used to form a concave base. At the apex he has sunk a nail on which to impale the staves. He criss-crosses eight to ten strips on

LEFT: *After loosening the wood with a mallet, Colburn lifts off the peel in annual layers.* RIGHT: *He strips the peel with a device having a row of razor blades embedded in the top at 1-inch intervals.*

DAVID ASGARD

this point so they radiate outward for nearly equal lengths and even distances. Now he presses a metal ring down where the staves cross, places a small wood block on top of this, and lowers a hinged brace from the ceiling. A threaded bolt has been sunk into the end of the brace. When this is turned, pressure is applied so this simple vise holds the staves in place at the point where they intersect. Before beginning to weave, Colburn splits one of the staves in half from the central point to the end. This results in an uneven number of staves, which can be alternated as he weaves the base.

The weaving is done by going over and under adjacent staves with a narrower rod or split.* Working from left to right around the base, when one split is exhausted, he lets in another and continues weaving. When he reaches the diameter of the proposed base (about 9 inches for a peck measure), the vise is released, the basket base removed, and Colburn is ready for the next step.

Many basket makers do not use a mold, but the Colburn method of making a basket around a solid, wooden form helps assure a uniform, even-sided product. The woven base is reversed now and set evenly on the concave end of the mold. He anchors the staves near their center point with nails driven through small squares of iron and into the form. Then Colburn drops a metal hoop over the radiating stave ends to keep them close to the sides of the mold. He inserts a metal bar into a hole in the opposite end of the mold and clamps this in a bench vise. This allows him to rotate the mold against his chest at an adjustable angle as he weaves.

---

* *The staves* in basket-weaving are stationary, like the warp in loom weaving (see photo 4). The *rod* (or *split*) in basket-weaving is like the weft or woof in loom-weaving. These are the pieces that are woven in and out of the staves. When one rod is used up, another is let in.

LEFT: *The base is woven on a low conical block.* RIGHT: *The woven base is then reversed and set on the concave end of the basket mold. A metal hoop keeps the stave ends close to the mold.*

DAVID ASGARD

Colburn weaves the sides with uniform-width splits (about ½ inch). When each is exhausted, he lets in another until the sides are about 7 inches tall.

Now the basket is slipped off the mold. Colburn has found that the more closely woven his basket is, the more difficult it is to remove from the mold. Sometimes he has to resoak it—mold and all—before the basket can be detached.

The ends of the staves must be trimmed and a rim made to finish off the basket and give it stability. Colburn does this by inserting one ring of black ash around the inside top circumference, another on the outside, and binding them to the stave ends with narrow strips plaited at even intervals.

Handles for the baskets can either be twin arcs opposite each other, or a single handle made from white ash or oak that arcs across the top of the basket. To make the double handles, Colburn soaks wide strips, inserts the shanks down through the rim and the horizontal woven strips, and bends up the ends to anchor the handles securely.

LEFT: *A metal bar inserted into one end of the mold is clamped in a bench vise. This allows Colburn to rotate the mold at an adjustable angle.* RIGHT: *Shaving a wood strip for a single-handle basket.*

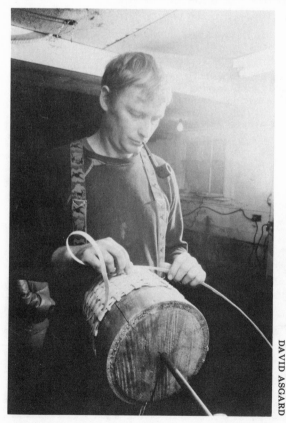

DAVID ASGARD

To make a single handle is more complicated. The wood of the desired dimension is steamed or boiled, then bent and anchored over a rack until it is dry. The ends of the handles are notched, tapered, and forced down into the weaving. The notches keep the handle from slipping out when the loaded basket is carried.

Colburn's finished baskets are made entirely of wood, with no nails or staples (the nails used in previous step are removed in order to slip the basket from the form). Their shape and the use of native material has been dictated by examples of baskets made by his father and grandfather in the same building. Colburn plans to continue the family craft.

"But there may be one hitch," he says. "That's the difficulty of finding a supply of black ash around here. With these small diameter trees, it takes an awful lot of pounding to work up a good supply of strips."

Painting Colonial Patterned Floors

Wooden floors painted with bold geometric designs were common in colonial America during the 1700s. Although evidence of original painted floors is hard to find today—unlike early stenciled walls and painted furniture, floors were subject to constant wear and have often been painted over, sanded down, or covered up—art historians can point to a few early American portraits and some family and business journals to confirm the popularity of this kind of home decoration.

Actually, floor patterns have been designed and executed for thousands of years. For centuries, geometric designs executed in mosaic, marble, quarry or ceramic tile, parquet, or any of the range of contemporary composition tiles, have added interest and color to floors in both domestic and public buildings.

When most people could not afford the luxury and comfort of imported rugs and carpets, painting patterns on wooden floors was one way to use native materials and copy fashion trends. Previously, home floor decoration was coupled with sanitation. Because raw wooden floors had to be scrubbed regularly, the earliest settlers used clean sand and a stiff broom frequently. In the best room of the house they often left a sprinkling of sand on the floor, working the sand into a pattern with their broom or a feather.

Whether executed by an itinerant craftsman or by the homemaker, a design painted on the floor was more permanent than sand, and could be done quickly by anyone who could handle a brush and use a measuring stick. It afforded the designer a chance for personal expression and was an inexpensive way to liven up a room.

Today, patterned floors can still mask patched or imperfect flooring in an old house or can be designed to simulate wide floorboards where none exist. And, of course, it is an authentic way to imitate colonial decoration.

David and Gerard Wiggins of Sanbornton, New Hampshire, are artisan brothers who carry on many of the traditions of itinerant craftsmen from past centuries. Recently they painted two patterned floors in the home of Mr. and Mrs. Roger Quigg, owners of the Andirons Inn in West Dover, Vermont. Using oil-based floor paints and commercial brushes, a chalk line, and a double-edged chisel for scoring the patterns on the floor, the Wigginses re-created a popular home decoration that flourished in eighteenth-century America.

The Wigginses also travel throughout New England retouching and reproducing old wall stencil patterns, decorating rooms with contemporary stencils of their own design, dealing in nineteenth-century genre and landscape painting, and following the family tradition of restoring houses and handling early American antiques.

The design they chose for the entry hall—a building-block pattern—is perhaps 3,000 years old. Executed in three colors, the pattern was copied from a mosaic floor on the Greek island of Delos. Often the same cube design—with variations in color and intricacy—can be seen in early American primitive portraits painted prior to 1800.

STEPHEN T. WHITNEY

A three-color "building-block" design based on a 3,000-year-old Greek mosaic floor. See diagram for pattern.

Squares, diamonds, and cubes were the most popular geometric forms used to decorate floors. They lent a degree of graciousness and opulence to a room. Often the designer "marbleized" or veined the paint while wet to enhance the illusion of a tile floor.

Usually floor patterns were carried to the baseboards; but in the Quiggs' dining room the decorator wanted a wide border left around the checkerboard design, to suggest the placement of a carpet in the center of the room.

The same type of design was used by another floor painter in the reconstructed and furnished parlor of the Prentis Collection at the New Hampshire Historical Society in Concord. There, the squares were slightly extended to form diamonds, which preserve the perspective over a large expanse (approximately 22' long × 17' wide) and make it appear even larger.

The patterned floors in the two rooms, although similar in conception, produced different effects.

David Wiggins' checkerboard design is made up of 15½-inch alternating brown and off-white squares. After establishing the size of the square in relation to the width of the floorboards, he and his brother snapped a chalk line to make diagonal parallel lines 15½ inches apart. Next, they did the same at right angles to these.

"One of the problems in the planning stage is to center the design in the room," Wiggins says. "This means a lot of measuring beforehand."

Once the pattern of alternating squares had been chalked, they scribed the design onto the floor with the double-edged chisel. This was drawn along the chalked lines but was not allowed to gouge and splinter the pine.

"Scribing helps you paint truer edges," Wiggins explained. This was the colonial method of keeping the paint in one square from running over onto another.

The Wigginses laid out the pattern on untreated pine boards. They gave each square two coats of paint and suggested the owners use it for several weeks before sealing the floor with two coats of polyurethane. Normal wear will take away the newness of a painted floor and tone it down to fit with its surroundings.

The floor in the New Hampshire Historical Society is painted on matched oak boards more than a foot wide. The pattern was painted in diamonds of black and off-white that measure 19¼" × 17½" from point to point. Each side of the pattern is 13 inches long. The paint was rubbed with the grain before it dried to bring out the texture of the oak floor. Then it was sealed. In this room the pattern runs to the baseboard on all sides and ends in half-diamonds along the perimeter.

More challenging to lay out, to paint, and to look at is the optical illusion created by the three intersecting lines of the block pattern, which the Wigginses used in the entry of the Vermont house.

Alternating black and off-white diamonds on this parlor floor (Prentis Collection, New Hampshire Historical Society) enhance the airy space of the room.

Scribing the floor was not possible because a continuous line would have overrun many of the geometric elements in the pattern. It was established instead with pencil on bare wood.

First, David Wiggins measured the width of the uniform floorboards and divided this by four. He took this measurement to run lines parallel to the joints between the boards from one end of the entry to the other, dividing each floorboard into four equal strips. Next, using the same measurement, he ran parallel lines at right angles to those already marked. This formed a grid of squares. Finally he drew parallel *diagonal* lines in one direction only, which bisected each square.

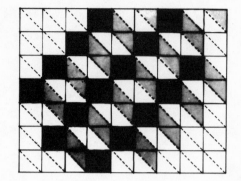

Layout for the building-block pattern shown at chapter opening—a gridwork of squares, with each square bisected by a diagonal.

The pattern is composed of squares and rhomboids—geometric figures whose angles are oblique and adjacent sides unequal. Unable to scribe the floor, Wiggins used short pieces of masking tape to keep the three paints where they belonged as he painted.

There are certain disadvantages to painted floors, whether patterned or plain. First, they must be retouched every few years if traffic over them is heavy. Second, elderly people may find sealed and polished painted floors dangerously slippery, and the patterns may prove confusing to persons with poor eyesight. Then, too, rooms without rugs generally have poor acoustics and tend to be drafty in cold weather.

Toward the end of the eighteenth century, this type of painted floor began to lose its appeal, and for a time stenciling was used to accomplish the job more quickly. Then floor cloths with painted overall designs were imported from Europe (costing far less than woven carpets) and they soon became popular. These cloths were successful in cutting down drafts, establishing more permanent designs, and adding purchase for the feet.

In the first decades of the young nation, taxes were levied against foreign imports to stimulate native industry. Soon Yankees were manufacturing not only their own floor cloths—heavy woven material that had been stiffened with sizing and patterned with paint—but rugs and carpets as well.

What many consider the most authentic colonial treatment of painted floors is the splatter paint method. Drops of different colored paints are sprinkled on a dried uniform background. According to historians, however, this method of floor decoration—first used on Cape Cod—was not found before the 1840s.

When patterned painted floors first became the vogue in this country is a question people like John F. Page, director of the New Hampshire Historical Society, hesitate to answer. Even the visual evidence of early portraits can be questioned as reliable sources. According to Mr. Page, one does not know whether the artist was

Two eighteenth-century floor designs from Nina Fletcher Little's booklet (see References). The left-hand design is for two or three colors, the right for two colors only.

recording an actual setting or was using his decorative talents to embellish the painting and make it more salable.

As affluence increased, fashions in floor treatment changed. But for a brief period in colonial America painted patterns on wooden floors decorated many homemakers' best rooms—from urban centers to outlying farmhouses.

REFERENCES

Nina Fletcher Little: "Floor Coverings in New England Before 1850," Old Sturbridge Village Booklet Series, 1967.
"The Prentis Collection," New Hampshire Historical Society, Concord, N.H.

About the Author

Richard M. Bacon and his family live as self-reliantly as possible on their small New Hampshire farm. Formerly a newspaper reporter and actor, he spent most of his professional life teaching at Collegiate School in New York City and Germantown Friends School in Philadelphia before a consuming passion for herbs and country living encouraged him to take up permanent residence and turn to farming and writing. A graduate of Williams College, he also studied in England at The London Academy of Music and Dramatic Art. He is the author of *The Forgotten Art of Growing, Gardening and Cooking with Herbs* and editor of *The Forgotten Art of Building a Stone Wall,* both published by Yankee, Inc., and has contributed articles to *Yankee, The Old Farmer's Almanac,* and *New Hampshire Profiles,* among other publications. Today, he and his family raise and process flowers for dried bouquets and sell herbs and herb products in the time left from tending a flock of sheep, geese, chickens, guinea hens, an all-purpose horse named Nellie Melba, and Maude, the family cow.